THE WESTWEG

THROUGH GERMANY'S BLACK FOREST

About the Author

Born and raised in Berlin, Germany, Kat Morgenstern discovered her passion for travel early on. At the tender age of 18, she left Germany to begin a journey that has taken her halfway around the world and is still in progress today. Professionally, Kat is a grassroots herbalist, ethnobotanist, writer and ecotravel professional. She is the founder and director of Sacred Earth, a network and educational resource for 'plant people' of all species, and of Sacred Earth Travel, a dedicated online ecotravel consultancy.

Having spent most of her adult life in the UK, the US and France, Kat currently makes her home in Germany's southern Black Forest, where she roams the hills and forests and has been surprised to find not only rewarding vistas and a great variety of ecosystems, but an innovative model of sustainable tourism development.

Other Cicerone guides by the author
Hiking and Biking in the Black Forest

THE WESTWEG

THROUGH GERMANY'S BLACK FOREST

by Kat Morgenstern

2 POLICE SQUARE, MILNTHORPE, CUMBRIA LA7 7PY
www.cicerone.co.uk

© Kat Morgenstern 2016

First edition 2016
ISBN-13: 978 1 85284 775 3

Printed by KHL Printing, Singapore
A catalogue record for this book is available from the British Library.

 Route mapping by Lovell Johns www.lovelljohns.com

Contains OpenStreetMap.org data © OpenStreetMap contributors, CC-BY-SA.
NASA relief data courtesy of ESRI.

All photographs are by the author unless otherwise stated.

Updates to this guide

While every effort is made by our authors to ensure the accuracy of guidebooks as they go to print, changes can occur during the lifetime of an edition. Any updates that we know of for this guide will be on the Cicerone website (www.cicerone.co.uk/775/updates), so please check before planning your trip. We also advise that you check information about such things as transport, accommodation and shops locally. Even rights of way can be altered over time.

The route maps in this guide are derived from publicly available data, databases and crowd-sourced data. As such they have not been through the detailed checking procedures that would generally be applied to a published map from an official mapping agency, although naturally we have reviewed them closely in the light of local knowledge as part of the preparation of this guide.

We are always grateful for information about any discrepancies between a guidebook and the facts on the ground, sent by email to updates@cicerone.co.uk or by post to Cicerone, 2 Police Square, Milnthorpe LA7 7PY, United Kingdom.

Front cover: High above the Murg Valley in the northern Black Forest (Stage 2)

CONTENTS

Acknowledgements

First of all I would like to thank the founding fathers of the Schwarzwaldverein, those early pioneers who recognised the value of their heritage and put so much effort into preserving it for future generations. Without their vision the Westweg would never have come to be – nor given rise to what is now an excellent and well-maintained trail network that comprises some 23,000km. In particular I would like to thank Herrn Patrick Schenk (Wegereferent), who has been most patient, generous and helpful in answering my many questions about the Westweg.

I would also like to thank Frau Gaby Baur and Frau Conni Karcher of Schwarzwald Tourismus for their kind support during the research phase of this project.

My heartfelt thanks also go to the tireless and hardworking people at Cicerone, foremost among them Lois Sparling, who never seems to sleep and is always so quick to assist and respond to my questions. My deepest gratitude, however, goes to Jonathan and Lesley Williams, for their encouragement and their belief in me. Thank you for your kindness, for taking this project on and for your wonderful company along a little part of the way.

Last, but by no means least, I would like to express my gratitude to my husband, Tino Gonzales, whose love and support is a constant source of inspiration to me. Thank you all for being part of my path!

Symbols used on route maps

～	route
⌒⌒	alternative route
Ⓢ	start point
Ⓕ	finish point
➤	direction
	woodland
	urban areas
	regional border
	international border
━■━	station/railway
▲	peak
	hotel/refreshments
♠ ⌂ ⋔	serviced/unserviced or partially serviced/picnic hut
⋏	campsite
■	building
	chapel or church/abbey
	castle or castle ruin
)(	pass
•	spot height
◗	grotto/cave
	ski lift/gondula
🛏	picnic area
▮SP	signpost
	observation tower/TV mast/wind turbine/s
	ski jumping ramp

Relief

Elevation
3800–4000
3600–3800
3400–3600
3200–3400
3000–3200
2800–3000
2600–2800
2400–2600
2200–2400
2000–2200
1800–2000
1600–1800
1400–1600
1200–1400
1000–1200
800–1000
600–800
400–600
200–400
0–200

SCALE: 1:100,000

0 kilometres 1 2
0 miles 1

Contour lines are drawn at 50m intervals and highlighted at 200m intervals.

GPX files for all routes can be downloaded for free at www.cicerone.co.uk/775/GPX.

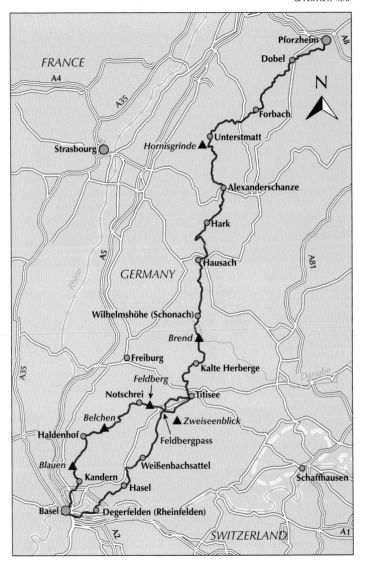

Wolfsgraben – one of many narrow gorges on the
southern fringe of the Black Forest (Stage 13B)

INTRODUCTION

Westweg Portal Schonach marks the beginning of Stage 8 at Wilhelmshöhe

In the far southwestern corner of Germany lies a small mountain range of worldwide fame: the legendary Black Forest, noted for its fairytale scenery and traditions, its cuckoo clocks, and most of all for its scrumptious gateau.

Yet the region has far more to offer than its well-worn clichés. The Black Forest, in the state of Baden-Württemberg, is one of Germany's most beloved walking destinations. The soft-contoured, forest-clad hills, interspersed with pastures and isolated farms snuggled into the folds of the mountains, and picturesque villages sprinkled among the hills,

make an ideal landscape in which to let both the mind and feet wander. The bald mountaintops – especially of the southern hills – offer a panorama of far-ranging vistas that not only encompass the soft ripples of the Black Forest, but on clear days can stretch right across the Alpine chain.

Comprising a total area of about 6000km² (about a third of the size of Wales), the region has an excellent infrastructure for walkers: about 23,000km of well maintained, way-marked trails, a very efficient public transport system and just enough conveniently placed benches, huts and farmhouse inns – often located in beautiful settings – offering not only physical sustenance, but also nourishment for the senses.

THE WESTWEG

Despite the fact that tourism development in the region started more than a hundred years ago, hospitality retains an authentic 'home-grown' feel. In part this is due to the early pioneering efforts of the Schwarzwaldverein. Founded in 1864 by a small group of innkeepers, the 'Schwarzwaldverein' (Black Forest Association) made it their task to promote and preserve the region's cultural and natural heritage, and to promote its appreciation by making it more accessible to tourists. They set to work immediately.

Their very first project was to establish a long-distance walking trail right across the entire length of the Black Forest that was to incorporate as many of the region's highlights as possible.

It was an ambitious project, spanning some 285km, from the 'Gold City' of Pforzheim in the north, to Basel in the extreme southwestern corner of the country, where Germany meets Switzerland and France, at the bend of the Rhine. The trail was to be clearly waymarked and well maintained, running high up and far away from towns and villages. Yet, it should provide enough shelter huts and hostels to make the experience safe and pleasurable for long-distance walkers who did not necessarily want to camp out.

By 1900 the task was complete. The Westweg (or The Westway in

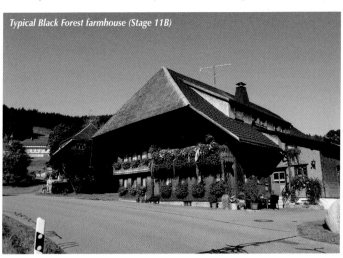

Typical Black Forest farmhouse (Stage 11B)

English) was inaugurated as one of Germany's first long-distance trails and it quickly became a hit. To this day its red diamond marker blazes the trail across the Black Forest and the route has lost none of its appeal.

The Westweg was soon followed by two other routes, the Mittelweg and the Ostweg, which also start in Pforzheim and run south to the Rhine, but neither ever managed to rival the Westweg's allure. It is the Westweg that reigns supreme for status and eminence among classic long-distance walks in Germany.

While the Black Forest covers a relatively small area and its peaks never exceed 1500m in height, the route nevertheless has its challenges. Although the trails and terrain are easy, there are some rather steep sections. Some stretches of trail run on broad forestry roads, while others amble on narrow and uneven or rocky paths through the woods, although none require any special technical skill or ability beyond endurance. However, weatherproof equipment and sturdy boots are a 'must', and walking poles may prove a useful aid.

The route, which can be divided comfortably into 13 or 14 day-sections, comprises a total of about 8000m cumulative altitude metres – and sometimes a thousand of those have to be overcome in a single day. For seasoned alpine trekkers or hill walkers that might not sound like much, but the average walker should not underestimate the challenge.

However, this being the Black Forest rather than a remote mountain wilderness, it is almost always possible to shorten any part of the route by taking public transport, or by breaking one section into two, according to one's personal stamina and ability. Also, for those who do not relish being weighed down by a heavy pack – fret not! Walking-without-luggage packages or luggage forwarding services are available for almost all sections of this route.

While the Westweg does not compete for thrill and adventure with more alpine routes, its quieter, bucolic charms are seductive to those who are romantics at heart.

GEOLOGY

Geologically speaking, the mountains of the Black Forest are quite old. The bedrock, consisting of granite and gneiss, originated from volcanic activity some 200 million years ago. Variegated sandstone deposits, known as Bunter, which can mostly be seen in the northern parts, have built up through the eons. Thick layers of calciferous material (Muschelkalk and Keuper) around the southern fringes of the massif bear witness to an age when the region was covered by an arm of the Tethys Ocean and pre-historic corals populated this warm-water sea.

Prior to the Eocene epoch the Black Forest and the Vosges Mountains were part of the same tectonic plate,

On top of the Black Forest with panoramic views all around (Stage 10A)

but due to the enormous pressures exerted on the earth crust during the formation of the Alps, the plate was stretched and pulled in opposite directions, which caused it to thin and eventually to crack. In a process that has lasted millions of years and is still in progress (at a rate of about 0.1mm per year), the 'graben' has sunk by about 4000m. At the same time the broken-off edges of the plates have lifted up, bringing ancient bedrock of granite and gneiss to the surface, while softer layers of Bunter, Keuper and Muschelkalk have eroded. The debris has collected in the plain and built up layer upon layer of sediments that have filled the fissure, which is why today there is no 4000m-deep 'Grand Canyon' between France and Germany.

The tiny mountain range of Kaiserstuhl, situated to the west of Freiburg, is geologically unrelated to the Black Forest and the Vosges. It was formed during the Tertiary period and represents the climax of volcanic activity in the Rhine Valley.

During the last ice age about 10,000 years ago (the Würm glaciation), glaciers covered the entire Black Forest, and they have left their distinctive mark on the region's topography: soft contoured hills and valleys and near-circular tarns at the base of ancient cirques. After the ice retreated, the land, freed of the weight, started to rise. It is still lifting today, but at such a minimal rate that the effect is offset by erosion.

Geographically, the Black Forest is divided into a northern/central and a southern part, although the dividing line is rather arbitrary. The northern/central part extends from Pforzheim at the northernmost tip to Freudenstadt in the east, and Offenburg in the west. The Kinzig valley, which connects these two towns, forms the 'boundary'. Regions to the south are considered part of the southern Black Forest, also often referred to as Hochschwarzwald (High Black Forest).

In the northern parts, the tallest peaks rarely reach more than 1000m above sea level. This area is characterised by seemingly endless miles of spruce-clad mountains, moors and deeply incised, steep and narrow valleys carved out by rivers that once were vital traffic arteries.

The southern Black Forest is where the tallest peaks are found, with Feldberg at almost 1500m topping the list. The southern edges of the massif are geologically still quite active – a phenomena that can be observed in the widening chasms of gorges, such as the Wutachschlucht.

The main central ridge of the mountains divides the region into an eastern and a western part. On the western flanks the mountains soar quite abruptly, rising up from the Rhine Valley to over 1000m, while the eastern slopes fall away much more gradually, forming an extensive high plateau that is characterised by gently rolling hills.

HISTORY

Despite its northern latitude, Baden-Württemberg bears many traces of extremely ancient human history. Some of Europe's oldest archaeological sites have been discovered at various locations between Stuttgart and Lake Constance, but the Black Forest has long remained a forbidding wilderness.

Evidence of early farming settlements dates to around 4000BC. Traces of such camps have been found at a number of locations, such as Schönberg near Freiburg, at Breisach am Rhein and Burkheim am Kaiserstuhl. But it was early Celtic tribes around 800–700BC that began to make inroads into the forest itself. Creating clearances on the eastern plateau near the source of the River Danube, they were the first to exploit the natural resources of the area – most notably its iron ore.

The Romans also had a significant impact on the region, especially around the southern and western edges, where remains of their villas can still be seen. After conquering Helvetia, now modern-day Switzerland, they pushed north along the Rhine, gradually usurping the Celts and driving them into the hills. By AD76 they had built the first traffic artery through the Kinzig valley, in the heart of the Black Forest.

The Romans, well known for their love of thermal baths, were delighted to find hot springs at sites such as Badenweiler and Baden-Baden and

Archaeologists digging for traces of Pforzheim's ancient past (Stage 1)

set about constructing elaborate bath houses. The original Roman ruins can still be seen today. Their traditions, meanwhile, have evolved into a modern spa culture.

As the Roman Empire went into decline by about the third century AD, their settlements in Germania became increasingly vulnerable to attacks by Alemannic tribes from the north. The Romans withdrew south of the Rhine and the once grand administrative centre of Augusta Raurica (only about 20km from modern-day Basel), which during its heyday was home to about 20,000 people, eventually reverted to the status of a small fishing village.

The first determined attempts to settle and 'civilise' the Black Forest came in the seventh century with the arrival of Irish monks, who were on a mission to evangelise the heathen outposts of Europe. Most of the grand and powerful clerical centres in the Black Forest, such as St Trudpert in Münstertal and St Blasien, originally started as hermitages. In their diligent effort to 'gain dominion over nature', the monks cut down the forest and built their pious outposts in the wilderness.

The forest, along with the silver mines that brought riches to cities such as Freiburg, was the livelihood of the then sparse population. Ancient tree giants supplied the building material for many of Germany's grand medieval churches and castles. In later centuries they were also bound for export to

Holland, where they were turned into the Dutch merchant fleet.

In the days before motorised transportation, moving the massive tree trunks to bigger rivers, such as the Rhine or Neckar, was a major logistic challenge. Spin-off trades related to the timber industry began to proliferate. Rafting, charcoal making, glass manufacture and potash production all boomed – and brought the forest ecosystem to the brink of collapse. Only the absence of heavy machinery and intermittent calamities, such as outbreaks of the plague or war, periodically halted the devastation and gave the forest a chance to recover. But at the dawn of the industrial revolution, tree cover had been reduced to only 30 per cent.

During the latter part of the 19th century circumstances conspired to bring about a radical shift. Firstly, the growing influence of industry on people's lives nurtured a new appreciation and idealisation of nature. The 'idea of nature' became the 'holy grail' of the Romantic movement and artists and philosophers revered nature as a source of inspiration.

The Black Forest was one of the first regions in Germany to discover its potential as a tourist destination, although at first it wasn't the forest or the mountains that attracted visitors from all over Europe, America and Russia – it was the allure of a cure. The numerous mineral-rich hot springs of the Black Forest, which had been praised for their

Rötteln Church, built on the foundations of one of the earliest Christian sites in the region (Stage 13A)

curative powers since Celtic times, now attracted the gentry of Europe. Once the first steam engine railway lines were introduced, the healing waters attracted an influx of well-heeled tourists, and became a lucrative source of revenue for the region.

Medical philosophy at the time also held that fresh air and gentle exercise, such as walking, was conducive to health and wellbeing. However, royalty could not be expected to roam the woods, so the solution was to create 'Kurparks' in every spa town: beautiful park-like arboretums, embellished with ornamental trees and bushes from far-flung regions of the planet, were created in the English style that was the fashion at the time.

In 1864 the now-famous Schwarzwaldverein (Black Forest Association) was founded with the idea of protecting the cultural and natural heritage of the Black Forest and promoting it to walkers and tourists. To this day, walkers are indebted to the efforts of these early pioneers. All the routing, waymarking and maintenance of the region's extensive network of walking trails is carried out by its members; in recent years the Schwarzwaldverein has also played an important role in the creation of the Naturparks Schwarzwald Nord and Schwarzwald Süd, mediating between various interest groups to safeguard sensitive habitats and cultural sites, while promoting sustainable outdoor

Latschigfelsen – a prominent promontory high above Murg Valley (Stage 2)

Burg Rötteln, near Basel, dates to at least the 13th century (Stage 13A)

activities. Thanks to these efforts the Black Forest has evolved into a flagship region for sustainable tourism in Germany.

PLANTS AND WILDLIFE

In January 2014 parts of the northern Black Forest were designated as Germany's newest national park, consisting of two separate pieces of land which together cover an area of about 10,000ha. These areas have not been set aside because of their innate wildness, but rather as an effort to 're-wild' them, and thus to provide better habitat protection for a number of endangered species that are native to the Black Forest. The effects will not be apparent during the initial stages of

rehabilitation as it may take 30 years or more for nature to reclaim her ground.

Mountains clad in tall, dark spruce and fir trees and a sombre atmosphere is the classic image that has given the region its name. For many centuries this image was not far from the truth, but today the ecosystem is changing. Originally the forest ecosystem consisted mainly of beech and oak, as well as silver fir (*Abies alba*), all of which are considered high-value timber species and sources of fuel. For many centuries the forest was fiercely exploited, and sadly, no stands of original primary forest have been preserved.

Attitudes did not begin to change until the time of the industrial

Trail through the predominantly deciduous woodlands of the southern Black Forest (Stage 12A)

revolution. Realising that overexploitation of forest resources was putting people's livelihoods at stake, the authorities passed the first legislation to protect the environment. It was decreed that no more timber should be harvested in any one year than could naturally regrow within the same period. Simultaneously, a massive reforestation campaign was launched.

Unfortunately, then as now, ecological considerations came second to economic priorities. The forest was stocked with fast-growing, commercially valuable Norwegian spruce and Douglas fir, which, thanks to their straight growth and sparsely branched trunks, soon returned a profit. The forest recovered remarkably quickly – within 60 years it had pretty much

replenished – but the economically biased strategy soon proved to be short-sighted: the forest had basically been turned into a monoculture of shallow-rooted trees. It was a disaster waiting to happen. And happen it did – most poignantly in December 1999, when legendary hurricane Lothar blasted its way across the Black Forest and within just a few hours lay waste to about 40,000ha of trees.

During major storms, trees with shallow root systems tend to fall like matchsticks. Of course, a storm with the ferocity of Lothar (gusts of over 200km per hour were measured on Feldberg) has the power to flatten anything. But the effect was particularly devastating due to the predominance of these types of trees. Even now, the aftermath of the storm can be observed on many exposed hillsides. It has transformed the terrain and galvanised a shift in forest management. Today more effort is invested in making the forest more climate resilient by planting a variety of species and especially more native deciduous trees. Gradually the forest is changing and returning to something resembling its original ecology.

The growing stands of mixed deciduous trees in the southern Black Forest have created an ambience that is quite different to that of the northern parts, where conifers still dominate and many storm-ravaged areas remain; where dead trees form bizarre sculptures amid young growth but open views still prevail.

Another typical landscape feature, especially in the northern mountains, are the patches of moorland, locally known as *Grinden* – the result of deforestation followed by regular grazing. Even though these moors essentially represent a degraded, man-made landscape, they provide a habitat for highly specialised plants and animals, such as sundew (*Drosera sp*), cottongrass (*Eriophorum sp*), marsh cinquefoil (*Comarum palustre*), bog bilberry (*Vaccinium uliginosum*), bogbean (*Menyanthes trifolia*), bog-rosemary (*Andromeda polifolia*) and various insects, including rare dragonflies that can only survive and thrive in such harsh and specialised biotopes.

At the higher altitudes conifers still dominate, while the understory layer consists of mosses and ferns that relish the humid atmosphere. This is the habitat of the endangered wood grouse. Heather, bilberry and cowberry are often found carpeting areas that have lost their tree cover due to

Left to right: left: Fly Agaric (Amanita muscaria); Yellow Gentian (Gentiana lutea); Moorland Spotted Orchid (Dactylorhiza maculata)

21

the ravages of hurricane Lothar. These open areas also provide a habitat for snakes, such as the European adder, while grass snakes tend to prefer a more boggy terrain.

At lower altitudes there is a richer diversity of tree species, which includes oak, beech, maple, hazel, willow, poplar, lime, mountain ash, and along the warmer western edges, sweet chestnut and even walnut. The understory here tends to be dryer, and occasional stands of holly can also be found. On the southernmost fringe near Rheinfelden, a small natural stand of box trees (Buxus sempervirens) is protected as a nature reserve.

Open meadows and pastures display the full range of central European flora, its variations dependent on soil composition and altitude as well as ecosystem characteristics. Habitat protection is patchy and sometimes covers just an individual field to safeguard specific plants or animals found only in a particular spot.

Perhaps surprisingly, larger animals are rarely seen. Deer, fox and wild boar tend to avoid humans, although they are there, and in recent years even the lynx has returned to its former range in the Black Forest. Birds are by far the easiest animals to observe, and thanks to the variety of habitats there is quite a wide range of species – including wood grouse, peregrine falcon, storks, three-toed woodpecker, green woodpecker, spotted nutcracker, kestrels, red and black kites, buzzards, haw finch, golden oriole, great grey shrike, red-backed shrike, black redstart, blackcap, yellow hammer, cuckoo, goldcrest, goldfinch and wagtails, to name but a few.

BANNWALD

Although the Black Forest is a managed environment, there are quite a few areas known as Bannwald (special protection areas) that are set aside for scientific study. They are neither managed nor cut, although if necessary the forestry service may clear obstructed trails. Thus, walkers should be especially careful of falling branches and other unsuspected dangers when entering a Bannwald. On windy days they are best avoided.

In protected areas (Naturschuzgebiet) special rules apply:

- keep noise down (ie no portable stereos etc)
- keep to the trails
- do not pick mushrooms
- do not collect stones or minerals
- do not feed the wildlife
- do not litter
- no open fires
- use official campsites
- do not remove plants or animals
- keep dogs on a leash
- do not fly model airplanes or kites.

WALKING THE WESTWEG

The Westweg leads from the northernmost outpost of the Black Forest in Pforzheim to Basel in the 'tri-country

Above the clouds on the Dobel plateau (Stage 1/2)

corner', where Switzerland, France and Germany meet. Starting in Pforzheim, the route follows the River Enz to Neuenbürg an der Enz, with its medieval castle towering above the town. From here it climbs up to the Dobel plateau. Although on the first day it takes a little while to leave civilisation behind, the second stage runs high above the towns and villages nestled in the valleys, with many beautiful, long-ranging views to the north and west. After passing through the nature reserve at Kaltenbronn, which protects the largest coherent upland moor in Germany, the trail heads down to the valley of the Murg, where the second stage ends in the picturesque town of Forbach.

The deeply cut valleys of the northern Black Forest are experienced on the third stage – one of the most demanding sections of the entire route. Some rather steep climbs add up to about 1000 cumulative altitude metres between Forbach and Unterstmatt, taking in the peaks of Badener Höhe (1002m), Hundseck (856m) and Hochkopf (1041m) along the way.

The fourth stage is relatively easy, and very scenic, although it's a long day's hike. After a steep climb to Hornisgrinde (1163m), the highest peak in the north, the trail runs along the central ridge via Ruhestein (997m) and Schliffkopf (1054m) to Alexanderschanze, with wonderful long-distance views for most of the way.

The following two days provide a complete contrast as the route runs almost entirely through the forest, with

Lake Titisee, the largest natural lake in the Black Forest region (Stage 9)

only occasional passages through open terrain and glimpses of the valleys below as the trail approaches Hausach in the Kinzig valley, which lies approximately at the midpoint of the route and also at its lowest point of elevation.

Hausach is the gateway to the central/southern Black Forest – a region of more open farmland and softer contours. But the climb back up to the ridge is pretty steep, and this stage tots up another 1000+ altitude metres on its way to Wilhelmshöhe. The higher mountains are getting closer now and the open long-distance views across the rolling hills lift the spirit – compensating for the fact that from Neueck to Süßes Häusle the trail runs rather close to the busy

B500. Thereafter, the panoramic vistas are unimpeded and a pure joy, almost all the way to Titisee – a busy tourist spot on the largest natural lake in the Black Forest.

In Titisee the trail splits and you have to decide whether to continue along the western edge of the massif, taking in some of the highest peaks – Feldberg, Belchen and Hochblauen – before descending through the rolling vineyards and orchards of Markgräflerland, or whether to take a more easterly route, via Herzogenhorn and Blößling to Todtmoos and the open farmland of Dinkelberg, to reach Basel.

Both routes are quite beautiful and each has its own highlights, but the western route is arguably the more interesting – and thus the more popular and busier of the two. The eastern branch is quieter, less dramatic (but not necessarily 'easier' in terms of altitude metres) and has more contact with towns and traffic along the way.

North to South or South to North?

Although the route is marked in both directions, almost everybody walks it from north to south – and with good reason. While the mountains are the same, the views are not. Walking from north to south, the anticipation grows as one approaches the higher hills ahead, and majestic Alpine peaks tower on the distant horizon. Basel, with its allure of cultural attractions and old-world charms, holds its own appeal as the final destination, whereas Pforzheim – well, lets just say it can't compete. But if all one wants to do is walk a small section, or some individual stages, the direction really does not matter much.

GETTING THERE

The Black Forest is very accessible and well served by a number of regional airports. If you are planning to start the Westweg in the north (recommended), the most useful airports to fly into are Stuttgart, Baden-Baden, or even Strasbourg, just over the border in France. If none of these are convenient, the next best international hub is Frankfurt. When you have completed the walk, rather than

returning to the arrival airport it would make more sense to fly out of Basel's Euroairport, or even Geneva or Zurich – especially if you're walking the full length of the trail.

Stuttgart airport (www.stuttgart-airport.com) is served by several airlines from various cities in the UK and Ireland and from all over the world. The S2 or S3 light railway lines connect the airport with the central station (Hauptbahnhof), from where a local train takes you directly to Pforzheim.

Baden-Baden is not the most convenient airport for getting to Pforzheim. However, it is a good option for those wishing to spend a little extra time exploring Baden-Baden. The airport is very small and schedules frequently change. Current flight information is available at: www.baden-airpark.de/startseite

There are several buses that connect Baden-Baden airport with other destinations. Hahn Express (www.hahn-express.de) connects it with Hahn airport (Ryanair's Frankfurt outpost), with stops in Baden-Baden and Karlsruhe. There is no direct service from Baden-Baden to Pforzheim; switch to a local train in Karlsruhe.

Thanks to its role as a political hub in Europe, Strasbourg airport (strasbourg.aeroport.fr/en) is reasonably well connected to many European cities, including London. Both a shuttle train and bus service connect the airport with the city centre several times per hour. A trans-border train

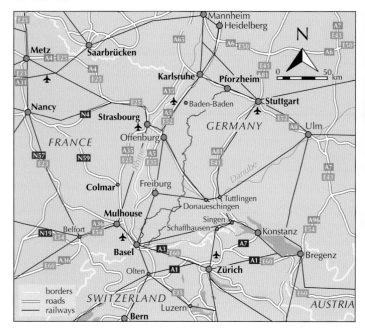

service departs from the central station to Karlsruhe, where local trains leave for Pforzheim.

Frankfurt (www.frankfurt-airport.com) is Germany's main international airport hub, served by every major airline. There is a train station right at the airport with direct (fast) trains to either Stuttgart or Karlsruhe, where local trains leave for Pforzheim.

Basel/Mulhouse (EuroAirport: www.euroairport.com/en) is well connected to many airports in the UK, Ireland and other parts of Europe. Since the Westweg ends in Basel it is a convenient airport to fly out of.

But beware – although the terminal is quite small, it can be a bit confusing. The terminal building is divided into a Swiss and a French side, each with its separate entrances, customs and passport controls. Be sure to know which side your flight departs from (or which exit you want to take, if you arrive here!).

Basel also has three train stations: the central station (Basel SBB), the French SNCF right next to it and Badischer Bahnhof on the other side of the Rhine, which is located on Swiss territory but run by the German train service, DB.

A regular airport shuttle bus (#50) runs between the central station (Basel SBB) and the airport (Swiss side). If you arrive here, don't take the French shuttle bus service, Distribus #11, as it only goes to the Gare SNCF in Saint Louis (the French part of Basel) and this would make your onward journey rather complicated.

The Swiss and German stations are connected by a local train service (S6), by tram (#2) and by bus (#30).

Should you arrive in Basel, the quickest and least complicated way to get to Pforzheim is to take the ICE (fast train) from Basel SBB to Karlsruhe and then switch to a local train to Pforzheim.

GETTING AROUND

If you start the Westweg in Pforzheim or Basel you should have no difficulty finding the trailhead. But if you want to walk only part of the way or explore individual sections as day walks, you should request or download the brochure 'Westweg mit Bus und Bahn' from the Black Forest tourist board (unfortunately only available in German) by going to www.schwarzwald-tourismus.info, placing your cursor on the 'Info' tab at the top of the page, and selecting 'Prospektbestellung'. Scroll down the page to get to the brochure, which includes a map showing the nearest bus stops for accessing various points along the route.

Wollbach village (Stage 13A)

See Appendix C for further information on route-planning and transport providers.

Konus card

Most hotels and guesthouses issue a 'Konus card' upon check-in (or check-out). This card is what you get for paying the local tourist tax. It entitles the cardholder to free public transport on local buses and trains throughout the Black Forest region, for the duration of your stay at each hotel. Even if you don't think you'll need it since you'll be walking, it is worth taking anyway. It allows you to shorten a section or change your plans if the weather suddenly turns, or if you are injured or sick – or if you just want to spend some time exploring other places nearby. It might mean a bit of extra paperwork at check-in, but at least it comes with benefits. If it is not offered, ask for it! To download more information about the Konus card, go to www.blackforest-tourism.com, place your cursor on the 'Info' tab at the top of the page, select 'sales guide' and scroll down the page to the brochure entitled 'KONUS – bus and rail for free'. (Not available in mayor towns such as Freiburg, Offenburg, Karlsruhe or Pforzheim.)

WALKING WITHOUT LUGGAGE

Many hotels in the region offer luggage-forwarding services for walkers who don't want to carry their own gear. This is a very convenient service, but

it does not necessarily come cheap – especially if the next accommodation is a long way by car. While the distance between one hotel and another 'as the crow flies', or in this case 'as the hiker walks', is usually relatively short, going up and down and around a lot of little mountain roads can take a long time and racks up quite a few miles. You may be looking at €10 to upwards of €20 per person, although some places charge less if a whole group of people all want their luggage delivered to the same place.

If you really hate carrying gear you can arrange the luggage forwarding yourself. Simply ask when booking your room whether the service is available and how much they charge; that way you can decide each day whether you want to carry your luggage yourself or use the service. (Some sections of the trail are a lot harder than others!)

Another possibility is to pre-book the whole tour, or parts of it, with both accommodation and luggage-forwarding service included. Check www.schwarzwald-tourismus.info for details.

WHERE TO STAY

The Black Forest is a well-established tourist region with a wide range of accommodation to choose from – in most places. However, Westweg has been routed to avoid villages as much as possible. While there are some simple guesthouses that lie directly on,

Alter Rabe guesthouse (Stage 8)

or very close to the trail, sometimes there is not a lot of choice and pre-booking is definitely recommended. If you are likely to arrive after 6pm at your accommodation it's a good idea to call and let them know.

Some hotels that do not lie directly en route may offer a free transfer from and to the trail. Ask at the time of booking.

When arranging your trip, keep in mind that Westweg is a popular route and the Black Forest is an extremely popular walking destination. During peak hiking season, in spring and autumn, pre-booking is essential.

The accommodation listing included in Appendix B; is not exhaustive, but presents a selection of the most convenient places. For further options check the village/town website, or the accommodation listing (*Gastgeber Verzeichnis*) at www.schwarzwald-tourismus.info.

Note that not all guesthouses take credit cards and ATM machines may not be available nearby.

Camping

There are many basic shelter huts sprinkled throughout the Black Forest, and theoretically it is possible to camp at these overnight. Wild camping is tolerated for one night 'if the walker is in need' – however, this regulation can be open to interpretation. Basically, the huts are meant for shelter in case of bad weather or as picnic huts for day-trippers. The forest warden can decide to send campers packing – or not – depending on his mood, or on the conduct of the prospective campers. The basic shelter huts are not exactly comfortable and only a few of them have sleeping platforms. Making a fire anywhere other than at designated grill places is prohibited.

Regular, serviced campsites can also be found throughout the region, however, there are almost none in the immediate vicinity of the trail.

FIRST AND LAST NIGHTS

Pforzheim

With only 120,000 inhabitants, Pforzheim is a rather small and sleepy town which was almost completely destroyed during WWII. The new town that sprang up in its place has all but lost the historic character. However, there are a few interesting museums (most notable is the museum of jewellery – www.schmuckmuseum-pforzheim. de) and the World Heritage site of Maulbronn Abbey (www.kloster-maulbronn.de) is only 30min away by public transport, if you happen to find yourself there a day early and are looking for things to do.

Unfortunately there are not a lot of recommendable hotels. The Parkhotel, located near the confluence of the rivers Nagold and Enz, is the best choice in town. However, this hotel serves as the hospitality hub for convention guests, as it is located right across from the convention centre. For less expensive options look for small *Landgasthaus* (country inn) or *Pension* (B&B) in nearby villages.

Rustic picnic huts offering basic comforts are sprinkled amply throughout the region

If you want to expand your trip to include a bit of culture, you might like to consider spending a couple of days exploring the beautiful historic spa town of Baden-Baden, which is only about 45min away by local train.

Basel

At the opposite end of the trek lies Basel, known as the 'Tri-Region City', which is to say that the urban area of Basel merges Swiss, French and German parts across the borders, due to their common, shared heritage. Basel is a buzzing university town as well as an ancient bishopric centre, although today it is best known for its pharmaceutical industry.

Although industry along the Rhine is quite intense, Basel manages to preserve a lot of charm, especially in the old town centre. It is well worth spending a little extra time here if your schedule permits, to soak up the lively atmosphere and visit some of the excellent museums and galleries.

There are many hotels, inns and B&Bs in and around Basel. The area around Badischer Bahnhof is not exactly pretty, nor centrally located, so it may be better to look for a place on the shores of the Rhine, in the old town (south of the river) or nearer the SBB train station, from where it is also easy to catch the bus to the airport. However, Swiss hotel prices can be steep. For more budget-friendly options look for a place in Lörrach, just across the border in Germany, only a short tram ride away from the town centre.

On most (but not all) sections, you will be able to find serviced huts or cafés/restaurants along the way. Hotels usually have a restaurant on the premises, but some types of guesthouses (*Pension*) do not. Some Schwarzwaldverein huts are only open on weekends and public holidays during the main hiking season. Restaurants often take their day off (*Ruhetag*) on Mondays, Tuesdays or Wednesdays. Thus, it is always a good idea to bring some supplies – squirrel away an extra sandwich and pack some fruit from the breakfast buffet, or ask for a lunchbox before heading out.

Those following a special diet, such as gluten-free, lactose-free, vegan or vegetarian, may find their options severely limited. Although most better restaurants offer at least a couple of vegetarian alternatives, it is best to check your options before you get there. Many restaurants will be happy to accommodate you if they know your requirements in advance, but don't expect to find multiple choices for non-traditional diets on the regular menu. For an explanation of certain regional food items, see the glossary in Appendix D.

Water

The importance of plentiful hydration cannot be stressed enough. In general, the Black Forest is a water-rich area and there are many public water fountains. Unfortunately, they often display signs giving a warning that their water is not potable ('*Kein Trinkwasser*'). What this usually means is that no-one actually comes to check the water on a regular basis to make sure it is safe for human consumption and thus, if you drink it, you do so at your own risk. To be on the safe side, fill your water bottle at your hotel or ask at a serviced hut, restaurant or farm.

DANGERS AND ANNOYANCES

As mountain ranges go, the Black Forest is quite 'civilised' and comparatively 'easy'. Trails are well maintained and clearly marked and the nearest village is never more than a few kilometres away. Even so, don't underestimate the mountains – however bucolic they may seem!

If the weather suddenly turns you may be lucky and find a shelter hut nearby, but if you get caught in a raging thunderstorm be sure to avoid seeking shelter in the observation towers (which were built at the top of many hills in the region about 100 years ago to provide views above the tree cover, and which are therefore rather vulnerable to lightening strikes!). On windy days falling branches can become dangerous projectiles, and after heavy rain mudslides and falling rocks can make hiking treacherous.

Wild animals generally are of little concern in the Black Forest. Of the bigger mammals only wild boar poses a potential danger to humans and dogs, but they tend to avoid contact if they can. They are most active at dawn and dusk. Their senses of smell and hearing are very acute but their vision is terrible, so you're more likely to startle them when walking very quietly. The most dangerous time to encounter them is when they are out foraging with their young; this used to be in late spring/early summer, but nowadays they find such a surplus of food that they may breed and have offspring at any time of the year.

There have been no reported cases of rabies in Germany since 2006 and large animals are rarely seen. Far more dangerous are the tiniest critters, such as ticks, which can carry Lyme disease or TBE (tick-borne encephalitis). Ticks generally inhabit the undergrowth and tall grasses in lower elevations up to 700m, but they have also been found at 1500m (in the Czech Republic). Walking on broad forest tracks poses no risk, but when walking through tall grass it is best to tuck in the bottoms of your trousers. Tick repellent is only effective for about 4 hours; outdoor clothes can be treated with permethrin, which is highly effective, but also highly poisonous. Vigilance is the best protection – wear light-coloured clothes that make it easier to spot ticks and always perform a thorough tick check at the end of the day. If you have been bitten, seek medical assistance immediately, especially if you notice the classic symptom of Borreliosis infection – the bull's eye rash.

Adders like to hide beneath blueberry and cowberry bushes

There are very few species of snakes in Germany, and those that do exist are endangered and rarely seen. One of them is the adder, which likes to soak up the sun – sometimes quite close to a trail. They don't attack unless they feel threatened, and most will escape without you even knowing they were there. However, you or your dog or child might startle them by suddenly getting off the trail and scrambling around in the blueberries. Incidents are very rare, and there have been no confirmed fatalities in the last 10 years or so. Nevertheless, snake-bites can be serious, even though the poison itself is not deadly. It affects the circulatory system, and people suffering from cardio-vascular problems, dogs, children and the elderly

are most at risk. To avoid trouble, stay on the trails and keep dogs on a leash. Adder habitat (such as around Schliffkopf) is often designated as a nature reserve, where getting off the trail and berry picking is prohibited.

WHEN TO GO

It is best to plan this walk for the main walking season, between April and November. Although the lower sections will likely be perfectly passable, even in March or November, hotels and restaurants along the route are often closed during the off-season.

Since the climate is not as reliable as it used to be, it has become more difficult to predict conditions. In general, spring and early summer (April–June)

Wolfsgraben in autumn (Stage 13B)

or autumn (September/October) tend to be the best months of the year. In spring the temperatures are pleasant and flowering meadows and blossoming orchards make for delightful scenery. September and October are often drier than the summer months, which can be hot and humid with frequent threats of heavy thunderstorms. In autumn the colourful foliage and morning fog rising from the valleys creates a special ambience. 'Inversions', when warm air at higher altitudes traps colder, moist air (fog) below, are a particularly delightful experience on autumn walks – so long as one is walking above the clouds, that is.

Alas, Germans also tend to favour spring and autumn for their walking holidays, which means that trails can be quite busy and hotel rooms may be surprisingly difficult to find at short notice.

The county of Baden-Württemberg is always the last to take its summer vacations and school is out until the middle of September. Thus, 'shoulder season' does not start until about 15 September. Note that 3 October is 'Reunification Day' – a national holiday and among the busiest times of the year. In spring, Easter, Whitsun and Pentecost are the busiest times for walkers.

PUBLIC HOLIDAYS IN BADEN-WÜRTTEMBERG

The number of public holidays differs between federal states. Baden-Württemberg observes the following public holidays:

New Years Day: 1 January
Three Kings: 6 January
Good Friday: varies
Easter Monday: varies
Labour Day: 1 May
Ascension Day: varies
Whitsun: varies
Corpus Christi: varies
German Unification Day: 3 October
All Saints: 1 November
Christmas Day: 25 December
Boxing Day: 26 December

You can check specific dates of the moveable holidays at www.schulferien. org/Feiertage/Feiertage_Baden_Wuerttemberg.html

Inversion weather: walking in the sunshine above the clouds

EQUIPMENT

The basic needs of walkers are pretty much the same anywhere and vary only according to the season. The smaller and lighter the pack, the happier a walker you will be.

Here is a list of useful items that are recommended:

- fast-drying outdoor clothing (two sets of everything)
- sun hat
- warm hat
- scarf
- gloves
- rain jacket and waterproof trousers
- fleece jacket
- gaiters (not essential, but helpful in wet weather)
- micro-fleece magic towel
- good, sturdy, well broken-in hiking boots (waterproof!)
- walking poles
- light trainers
- refillable water bottle
- lunchbox
- energy bars
- sunscreen
- sunglasses
- first aid kit (plasters/blister plasters, disinfectant, bandage)
- personal medications you may need
- tick removal kit
- insect/tick repellent
- camera and charger
- maps and guidebook
- mobile phone and charger
- adapter plug
- whistle
- umbrella
- torch
- compass (optional)

It may seem ridiculous to pack a warm hat, scarf and gloves in summer, but the weather can change unexpectedly and you'll be glad to have them when you need them, which could be at any time.

MAPS, NAVIGATION AND GPS

Maps

The most useful map for the Westweg is the Leporello map, at a scale of 1:50.000. Leporello maps are a bit odd in that they tack each bit of the way below the previous section, showing just a little bit of what lies east or west of the route, and the whole thing unfolding like an accordion. The scale is a bit small, but it still shows a surprising amount of detail as well as providing additional information, such as a brief route description (in German), hotels en route, places to eat, local tourist offices, museums and bus stops. The map is laminated, which makes it waterproof and tear resistant. It is available from the Black Forest Tourist Board (see Appendix C for contact details).

Kompass also publishes a map specifically for the Westweg. Like the Leporello map it uses a scale of 1:50.000, is laminated and provides some helpful additional information.

A bit more expensive is the Schwarzwaldverein map set for the Black Forest, consisting of five maps (Freizeitkarte 501, 502, 503, 506, 508) and a planning brochure that gives some additional information about the route and accommodation options. The Schwarzwaldverein maps are not laminated and are thus more vulnerable to wear and tear. The scale is also 1:50.000.

The Schwarzwaldverein also publishes maps at a scale of 1:35.000, but given the mostly excellent waymarking all along the route, such detailed maps are not really needed.

The Kompass and Leporello maps are available on Amazon, and walking maps are also available at bookshops, tourist offices and often newsagents in the region. The Schwarzwaldverein Westweg map set is available from their online shop: www.swvstore.de

In order to comply with the criteria stipulated to certify as a 'quality hiking trail', Westweg was rerouted in 2012. Maps printed prior to 2012 – and even some that were printed in 2013 – do not reflect these changes (which are mostly minor but could lead to confusion).

Navigation and signage

About a decade ago the Black Forest trail system underwent an extensive reform. Previously, markers of every shape, size and colour proliferated on every other tree. The trail system has since been condensed and simplified. Now there are basically three distinct

A typical hiking signpost on Westweg

'You have only truly experienced the places that you have explored on foot' (Stage 7)

types of markers, almost all of which take the form of a diamond. (But just to confuse matters, some local areas have hung onto their old signs and routes, which may not coincide with the new system.)

The Westweg marker is a solid red diamond on a white background, which is also the logo of the Schwarzwaldverein. (Note that the Mittelweg trail symbol is a red diamond with a white line through its centre.) Despite the fact that Westweg is extremely well marked and generally quite easy to follow, there are still a few spots where the marking is ambiguous, missing or counterintuitive. The trail may amble along on a broad forestry track, when suddenly a half-hidden marker may point to a tiny little trail that heads off through the bushes. Or, there are spots where the route splits into a couple of variants, offering walkers a choice. The present book describes all the official variants that were marked at the time of writing, but these things can change – another reason why it is important to carry a current map.

Local trails are marked with a yellow diamond on a white background, while blue markers indicate regional routes. Long-distance routes have their own symbols, often composed of two different colours or a solid background with a logo in the centre. Trails often converge for a while before going off on their own again. Signposts are placed at important intersections, often holding many blades pointing in different directions. One blade at each signpost will usually show the name of the current location and its elevation. If there is more than one signpost in a given town or location, the name will follow the format 'name of town'/'specific location' – eg Pforzheim/Kupferhammer. If you use a Schwarzwaldverein map these names are shown next to the little yellow flags that mark the signposts.

The little symbols next to the various destinations indicate what you might find at a given location – eg bus stop is a green 'H' in a yellow circle;

a train symbol indicates a train station, the star or half-star a viewpoint. From one signpost to the next only the markers guide the way. Watch out for these little plaques or stickers! Some (fortunately not many) may have become overgrown, paled to obscurity or been placed in patently stupid places where nobody would ever think to look. Sometimes you have to chance walking down a trail for a few metres before spotting the plaque. Sometimes looking back might provide that reassuring clue, as the marker may have been placed more obviously for people coming the other way. As a general rule, keep your direction unless a marker points you to another trail.

Be aware that sections of the trail may occasionally be closed due to tree felling (especially in the autumn) or trail clearing after a storm. In such cases there is usually a banner barring passage, or a sign that reads something like *ACHTUNG WALDARBEITEN* and *LEBENSGEFAHR* ('Attention forestry works' and 'Danger to life'). On major trail routes such as the Westweg, a diversion is usually signposted – although in rare cases it may not be! A map will come in handy to figure out an alternative route.

GPS navigation

GPS navigation systems seem to have become the norm. While they can be helpful in pinpointing your current location, it is difficult to get 'the big picture' on such a tiny screen – if you can see anything at all with the sunlight glare, that is. However, it is not a good idea to rely exclusively on such electronic devices, as signal coverage is not 100 per cent. GPX tracks are available as free downloads from www.cicerone.co.uk/775/GPX

TRAIL ETIQUETTE

German walkers tend to be friendly and usually greet one another on the trail. If someone greets you with *Guten Tag* or *Grüß Gott* it is considered good manners to return the gesture, even if you only mumble a 'hello' in passing.

Some trails are shared between walkers and cyclists. Walkers have the right of way, but beware of mountain bikers, who sometimes come tearing down those forest roads at high speed. Fortunately they make a lot of noise. To avoid accidents it is best to get out of the way. Sadly, many mountain bikers do not respect the rules when it comes to the smaller footpaths, which technically are off limits to them. Confrontations do happen, as walkers tend to get extremely upset about this sort of thing.

LANGUAGE

The official language of the region is German, but the local dialect bears little semblance to what you might have learned at school. It is more like Swiss or Austrian German. (The dialect is known as 'Alemannic' and some linguists consider it a separate language.) Most young people speak at least some English.

TELECOMMUNICATIONS

For safety reasons, carrying a mobile phone is definitely recommended – but keep in mind that the Black Forest is not yet completely covered with mobile phone base stations and it is not uncommon to find yourself without a signal. However, towns and villages are usually covered.

Most (but not all) hotels and guesthouses now have wi-fi, but don't assume it will necessarily work in your room.

As of 30 April 2016, roaming charges within the EU have been significantly reduced (to basic domestic call rate plus 0.05c per minute), and from June 2017 they are going to be dropped altogether. Providing Britain is still in the EU at that point in time, roaming will no longer be the cost factor it once was. Otherwise, you might want to consider getting a pre-paid German SIM card. (eg FONIC), or check to see what kind of international options your mobile service provider offers.

Making local calls

You would be lucky to find a working phone booth anywhere other than at train stations. To make local calls with your mobile phone you may have to include the country code: 00 49, followed by the local code, but dropping the initial '0'.

The same applies to making calls to the UK, or anywhere else, including mobile numbers: 00 44 (UK) followed by local code without the initial '0'.

Emergency numbers

Police/Emergency: 110
Fire brigade/Ambulance: 112
Poison helpline: 0761 192 40

In areas where the trail traverses dangerous terrain there are usually signs nailed to the trees with the phone number of the local *Bergwacht* (mountain rescue service) and a code number that refers to the *Rettungssektor* (rescue sector) of the current location. Being able to provide this information to the search and rescue team greatly increases the chances of getting help quickly when needed.

HEALTH AND INSURANCE

Medical assistance

When setting out on a trip abroad it is always a good idea to check your health insurance coverage. EU citizens (which at the time of writing includes UK citizens) are covered for basic medical assistance in Germany. Apply for a European Health Insurance Card (EHIC) E111 – forms are available at the post office and on the NHS website; allow a few weeks for the application to be processed. When visiting a doctor's office you need to show the card and fill in a couple of forms to verify your eligibility and declare that you did not come to Germany specifically for the purpose of receiving treatment. Only basic dental care is covered under the health care system in Germany and surcharges must be paid for directly. If you incur any extra medical expenses, keep the receipts and try to get them refunded through the NHS or your private health insurance.

Vaccinations

No special vaccinations are required when entering from another EU country, but check that your basic immunisations are up to date, especially tetanus. You might want to consider a TBE vaccination, which is administered in a three-step schedule (plan ahead!). Ticks are active throughout the year, but spring and early summer is when they are most prolific. (TBE vaccinations protect against tickborne encephalitis, but **not** against Borreliosis!)

Insurance

Most regular travel policies do not cover adventurous activities such as walking or trekking – let alone mountaineering – so it's a good idea to take out specialist travel insurance. While few of us think of walking as a particularly risky pastime, accidents can and do occur, and the small cost of insurance is well worth the peace of mind of knowing that you will be covered even for things like emergency rescue and repatriation (which can be very expensive).

The Austrian Alpine Club (aacuk.org.uk) includes special insurance cover in its membership fees. This should amply cover anyone walking in the Black Forest.

Germany uses the Euro (€). Most small towns have banks or ATM machines that accept Cirrus, MasterCard and Visa; however, many shops and even some restaurant or small hotels only accept 'Eurocard' or cash. Westweg does not pass through many towns, so it's a good idea to carry sufficient cash.

It is almost always possible to find both cheap and expensive options for things like accommodation or food. Services are generally of a high standard and somewhat less expensive than in the UK. The cost of food can vary hugely: some of Germany's top gourmet restaurants are found in small villages in the Black Forest, while there are also plenty of rather basic eateries offering standard fare at reasonable prices. Hotel prices range from approximately €50–€130 for a double room per night (usually with breakfast included) and a decent dinner can be had for €20–€50 per person, depending on your appetite and penchant for gourmet meals.

It is customary to leave a small tip at better restaurants.

TOURIST INFORMATION

Germany's tourist infrastructure is excellent and the Black Forest is no exception. Most small towns have a tourist information office (look in the town hall or *Rathaus/Kurhaus*), which will often have some information available in English. Tourist offices also offer advice on walking routes, accommodation, restaurants and public transport, and many sell their own maps of the immediate region.

See Appendix C for tourist information contact details.

USING THIS GUIDE

The route description for each stage of the walk is preceded by an information box containing the following essential data: start and finish points; distance in kilometres; ascent and descent in metres; estimated walking time (this does not include refreshment and photo stops, so you should allow extra time when planning your day); refreshment options on the route; and any information about public transport and access that may be useful.

Within the route descriptions, text in blue italic indicates a named signpost (generally not shown on the stage map) that is important for navigation.

Text in **bold** indicates a feature that is passed on the route and marked on the corresponding stage map, and which often is also the name of the signpost at that location.

The stage maps have been reproduced at a scale of 1:50,000 and should be used in conjunction with the route description. These, along with printed maps or GPS information, should help you make sense of what you see on the ground. Also included are profiles of each stage of the route, showing the climbs involved.

Appendix A – a route summary table – gives at-a-glance statistics that will help in the planning of your walk. Appendix B provides a selection of accommodation providers, in route order, and their contact details. Appendix C provides further information and contact details that may be useful in planning or along the way, and Appendix D comprises a German–English glossary of terms and phrases that you might need on the Westweg.

PFORZHEIM TO HAUSACH

Hohloh Turm – the view from the top is decidedly better than the view at ground level (Stage 2)

STAGE 1
Pforzheim to Dobel

Start	Pforzheim station or Kupferhammer trailhead
Finish	Schulhaus (school), Dobel
Distance	24.6km via Schloss Neuenbürg; 23.8km via Höhenweg variant
Ascent	705m via Schloss Neuenbürg; 680m via Höhenweg variant
Descent	265m via Schloss; 250m via Höhenweg variant
Time	7–8hr
Refreshments	Many options along the way
Public transport	Pforzheim can be reached by local train (for example from Karlsruhe or Stuttgart). Several buses run from the bus terminal at the train station to Kupferhammer.
Access	As the first stage of the route is quite long you will need to spend the night prior to starting the walk in Pforzheim in order to get to the trailhead early and arrive in Dobel at a reasonable time. Alternatively you can shorten the route by taking the local train S6 up the Enz valley and start your walk in Birkenfeld or Neuenbürg.

It is about 2.5km from the station in Pforzheim to the official trailhead at Kupferhammer. Kupferhammer can be reached by bus (bus stop Kupferhammer), or on foot via a scenic route through town.

Since Westweg was re-routed some years ago, the first stage now splits at Unterer Enzsteg and rejoins at the adventure playground (Abenteuerspielplatz) by the school in Neuenbürg. The new, more scenic route runs through Neuenbürg an der Enz, via the castle (now a museum) that towers above the town. This route is a little longer and harder, as the trail first climbs up to the castle, then down again into the old town of Neuenbürg (on cobblestones) before climbing up the steep hillside to Abenteuerspielplatz, where the two routes meet again.

The old route (high route or Höhenweg), which is included here, crosses the Enz at Unterer Enzsteg and takes a slightly more gradual ascent via Birkenfeld. Once up above the valley the trail runs fairly level along the hillside, bypassing the old town of Neuenbürg altogether. The drawback is that one has to deal with more traffic and negotiate a busy roundabout in order to reach Abenteuerspielplatz.

After Neuenbürg the trail climbs, gently at first, to Straubenhardt, then more steeply up to the Dobel plateau. Just before reaching the end of the first stage the trail passes a mysterious chaos of boulders known as 'Volzemer Stein'.

PFORZHEIM

Pforzheim's marketing name, 'Goldstadt', has a glamorous ring to it that is somewhat deceptive. The name is derived from the city's history as a centre of jewellery manufacture. In 1767, the Margrave of Baden had given permission to the Dominican Order to establish a jewellery factory for the purpose of providing work for the inmates of its orphanage and 'home for the mad'. Apparently the inmates were quite talented and Pforzheim soon gained a reputation as the premier manufacturing centre for commercial jewellery and watchmaking in Germany.

However, contemporary Pforzheim is not famous for its charms. The plain, modern façades belie the city's ancient origins, which date back to Roman times. Founded in AD90, it was known as 'Portus' (river crossing, harbour) – a reference to its location at the confluence of the rivers Enz, Würm and Nagold. Naturally it became an important trade centre for the timber industry and rafting business, from where the Black Forest giants were floated down to the Rhine for export to destinations further afield. But with the advent of steam engines and railway lines at the end of the 19th century, the rafting business quickly ceased.

An air raid pretty much levelled the historic town centre on 23 February 1945. Unfortunately, unlike other towns that had suffered a similar fate, Pforzheim was rebuilt quickly, in typical minimalistic post-war fashion.

Museums

Schmuckmuseum (Museum of Jewellery): Jahnstraße 42, 75173 Pforzheim, **www.schmuckmuseum.de**

Schmuckwelten/Mineralienwelten (showroom of contemporary jewellery design and precious stones): Westliche Karl-Friedrich-Straße 56, 75172 Pforzheim, info@schmuckwelten.de, **www.schmuckwelten.de**

Technisches Museum der Schmuck- und Uhrenindustrie (technical museum for jewellery and clock-making industry): Bleichstraße 81, 75173 Pforzheim, **www.technisches-museum.de**

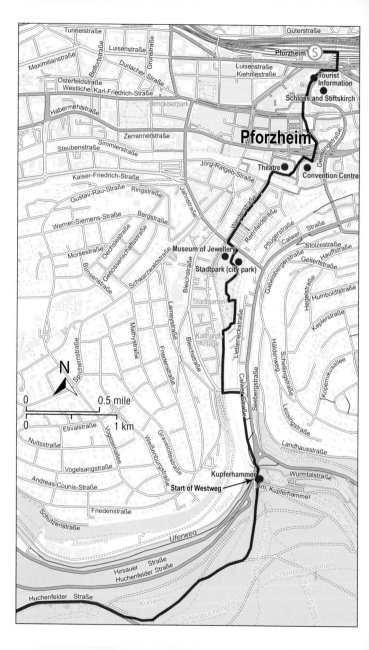

The tourist signposts list Kupferhammer/Wanderwege as a destination and Westweg markers also soon start to appear. Starting at the station, you can bypass the traffic chaos by using the subway to the left. Walk downhill on Schlossberg and just after passing the **tourist information** take the steps down to Marktplatz. Cross the square and head for the modern building opposite to find the stairs that lead up to the footbridge across the busy main road. Pass between the **Convention Centre** and **Stadttheater** (theatre) and cross the River Enz via Goldschmiedsteg (footbridge). Just to the left is the confluence of the Rivers Enz and Nagold.

Walk along the little canal down Werderstraße to Jahnstraße. Cross the road and pass the **Museum of Jewellery** to the left. Follow the River Nagold through the park (Stadtgarten). Cross the bridge (Kallhardtbrücke) and continue on the left-hand side of the river. Follow the footpath around the roundabout and cross Kupferhammerbrücke at the confluence of the rivers Würm and Nagold. Cross the road (B463) at the traffic light to find the trailhead just to the right of Kupferhammer Inn at **Kupferhammer**. ▶ (If you arrive by

Dating back to 1663, Kupferhammer is the site of an historic copper mill, which evidently was an important landmark at the time.

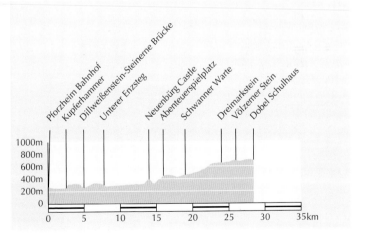

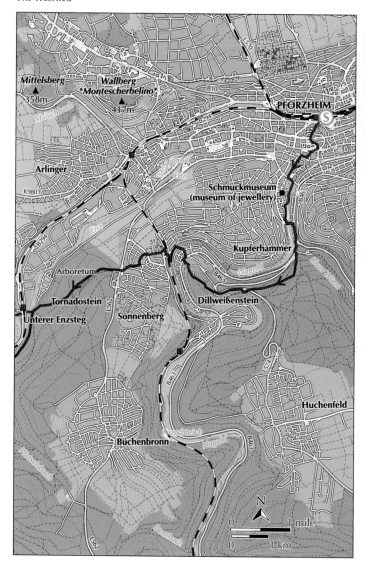

bus, walk towards the roundabout and cross the bridge – confluence of Würm and Nagold – to find the inn at Kupferhammer.)

Kupferhammer – start of the Westweg

By the edge of the forest, a wooden gateway – a so-called Westweg– Portal marks the trailhead. This is where Westweg (285km), Mittelweg (233km) and Ostweg (240km) set off on their way south. Westweg and Mittelweg start off together, while Ostweg takes a different route right from the start.

You will find these **portals** at the beginning and end of each 'official' stage. Information boards highlight the special points of interest along the way, and provide details regarding distances and the altitude profile of the stage ahead. A metal inlay on the floor outlines the whole route. Each portal has a little stamp machine, and the tourist office provides cards that walkers can use to collect stamps at each portal they pass. At the end of the journey, when

Map continues on page 53

49

the card is filled with stamps, you can take it to one of the major tourist offices and collect a souvenir – currently a Westweg headband.

After passing the portal the trail immediately starts climbing up through the forest, past the Auerbach monument.

This monument commemorates **Ludwig Auerbach**, the son of one of Pforzheim's most eminent jewellery manufacturers. Although his deepest wish was to become a poet, he obliged his father and took over the jewellery workshop, which, alas, he ran into ruin. He died young and unfulfilled, but one of his poems – 'Oh Schwarzwald mein' – is still celebrated as a kind of 'national anthem' of the Black Forest.

The trail crosses a little forest road and then bends to the right, towards a trail crossing. Cross Alte Huchenfelder Straße and continue straight on. Soon the trail reaches Huchfelder Straße.

Cross the road to *Hoheneck*, where Westweg and Mittelweg part company. Follow Westweg to the right, past the site of a medieval castle (not much to see now) and down towards the road. Turn left, past Landgasthof Hoheneck and head back into the forest.

At first the trail runs parallel to the road and passes a barrier. After passing some allotments it bends to the right and splits. Keep to the left (not clearly marked), passing more allotment gardens. At the other end of the hill the path reaches some steps and zigzags down to Hirsauer Straße (B463) in **Dillweißenstein**. Cross the road and bear right to the next corner, then turn left on Ludwig Platz. Cross the narrow bridge (*Steinerne Brücke*) and turn left along the River Nagold.

After about 150m watch out for a marker that points to a small path leading up to the road (easy to miss). Cross the railway tracks and walk up the stairs on the other side. At the top cross the car park and pass the cemetery to the left on Am Dillsteiner Kirchhof. Cross Auf der

Rotplatte and turn right. At the next corner turn left on Adolf-Becker-Straße. At the end turn right on Schultheiss-Trautz-Straße and at the T-junction turn left on Julius-Naeher-Straße. At bus stop Sonnenberg Steig 1 cross the road and bear left, then take the subway opposite Hotel Gasthof Sonnenberg to reach a small car park on the other side of the big road.

Cross the car park to *Sonnenberg* and follow Wasserleitungsweg Grösseltal (middle track) through Büchenberg **arboretum** to **Tornadostein**.

Tornadostein commemorates a **tornado** that swept through France and Germany on 10 July 1968, cutting a swath through the countryside half a kilometre wide and almost 100km long, which laid waste to an area of 700ha, including almost 30ha of trees.

At *Tornadostein* fork to the right and head down to the River Enz to reach **Unterer Enzsteg**, where Westweg splits into two variants: the main route via Neuenbürg Castle, or the old route via Höhenweg (see below).

For the main route turn left along the river. Soon after passing a footbridge, Westweg forks to the right. Cross the little street and continue straight on. After crossing a ford the trail splits; take the right-hand fork, past the pastures and keep to the right at the next fork as well.

Pass **Eberhard-Essich Hütte** and continue along the river on Bozenhardt Pionier Weg until the trail leaves the forest and passes underneath three bridges. By the allotment gardens take the small trail up the steps to reach *Neuenbürg/Eisenbahnbrücke*. After passing the allotments the trail meets another track at *Neuenbürg/Bahnhofsweg* and joins it to the left. The trail then reaches a paved lane and turns right, past the walkers' hostel (Wanderheim am Schlossberg), then follows the footpath up through the trees to reach the **castle**.

The oldest parts of **Neuenbürg castle** date back to the 13th and 14th centuries, but the hill was already occupied by a Celtic settlement during the fourth

Neuenbürg castle

and fifth centuries BC. However, the earliest traces of human habitation date back as far as 2000BC.

Walk around the ruin and pass the walled castle gardens to reach the 'new' castle at *Schloss Neuenbürg* (390m), which houses a museum. Follow the steep cobblestone walkway down to the centre of **Neuenbürg**.

Pass the church to the right and cross the street. At *Neuenbürg/Marktplatz* bear right and follow the road around to the left, across the river. Turn right on Alte Pforzheimer Straße, then fork left and follow Hafner-Steige steeply up the hill. At the top bear left in front of the apartment buildings and head into the woods, where several paths start. Westweg takes the middle trail to the left and soon after forks to the right to climb further up the hill to *Neuenbürg/Kindergarten*. Pass the kindergarden to the left, still going up the hill, and follow the left bend on Ludwig-Jahn-Weg. At the top join Scheffelstraße to the right to reach *Neuenbürg/ Abenteuerspielplatz*.

Old route via Höhenweg (high route)

At **Unterer Enzsteg**, turn right and cross the bridge and the train tracks. Bear left and cross the road at the pedestrian crossing. Start walking up the one-way street (Hohwiesenstraße) and look for the footpath on the left that leads steeply up the hill. At the top turn left on Baumgartenstraße and left again at the first corner. Take the footpath immediately to the right that leads through backyards and orchards to *Birkenfeld/Rathaus*.

Cross the road by the market square (Zeppelinstraße) and bear left past the police station to Rathausgasse. Turn left and head up the hill towards the forest. From here the trail runs more or less level along the edge of the hillside. At *Beim Schwarzwald Pavillion* fork to the right. ▸

Keep to the left and walk straight past Scheiterhau and Eichwald. Just before the barrier, turn left and

Map continues on page 55

Schwarzwald Pavillion is the hut just a few metres past the signpost – a nice picnic spot overlooking the Enz valley.

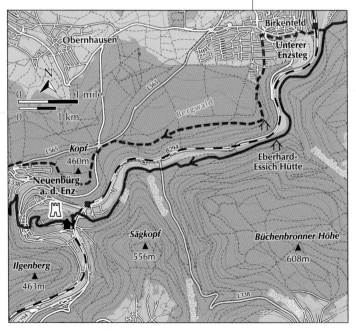

continue on the small trail parallel to a road (L565). After about 300m cross a road (K4541) and turn left at *Riegertswasen*.

By the wooden sign for Kopfrundweg, Westweg turns off to the left and soon reaches the outskirts of **Neuenbürg** (*Wilhelmshöhe*). Pass behind the houses to Vogelsangstraße; bear right towards the country road (L338a) and follow it to the left towards the big roundabout. Go around the roundabout and turn off on Albert-Schweitzer-Straße. Pass the school and miniature golf course to reach *Neuenbürg/Abenteuerspielplatz*, where the two branches of Westweg merge again.

From *Neuenbürg/Abenteuerspielplatz* follow Feldbergstraße, and after the traffic isle continue on the gravel path heading into the forest. After passing *Ob der Straße and Bergsträßle*, the path briefly touches the road by a lay-by. Cross the lay-by and follow the paved lane back into the forest, now mildly uphill.

By Schützenhaus turn left past the outskirts of Straubenhardt on a very scenic track along the edge of the forest, with far-ranging views towards the Swabian Jura to the east and the Palatinate Forest in the northwest. At **Schwanner Warte** – an observation tower maintained by the Schwarzwaldverein – cross the road and follow the trail to the left of Friedenslinde, back into the forest. ◄

Planted in 1871, Friedenslinde marked the end of the war with France and was intended as a symbol of hope for lasting peace.

Continue straight past *Herzogenwiese* (nature reserve) to a big trail crossing, where several trees are covered with huge tree fungi. Keep going straight up the hill to *Bücherweg*. Here Westweg branches off the broad forest track and continues on a smaller path to reach a gravel track at a bend. Follow the gravel track to the right, around the bend and straight on for about 1km. Look out for a marker unexpectedly pointing to a small path to the left; follow this trail to reach a hut and picnic area near a road.

Dreimarkstein, the ancient boundary stone that marks the borderline between the communities of Dennach,

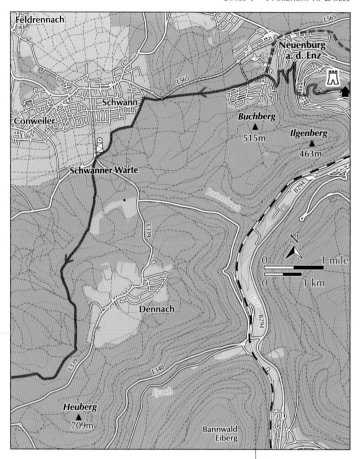

Conweiler and Dobel, is not the big boulder by the road, but a small stone near the picnic hut.

By the road at **Dreimarkstein** take the broad track (Hüttwaldweg) through the forest. After about 1.4km, like the long-forgotten remains of a sunken city, quite unexpectedly a jumble of boulders appears.

Map continues on page 57

*Dreimarkstein –
ancient boundary
stone*

Völzemer Stein is a jumble of Bunter sandstone
boulders – the result of erosion. Over the millen-
nia water has penetrated the tiny cracks between
the stones, and after eons of alternating cycles of
freezing and thawing it has cracked the rocks and
washed the softer sediments between them away.
Before being declared a natural monument in 1946,
locals used the site as a quarry for making mill-
stones or water fountains.

The trail emerges from the forest at **Enges Türle** and
reaches the outskirts of Dobel. Continue straight past the
field and turn right by the leisure centre (Freizeit und
Jugendheim) to reach the main road. Follow Neuenbürger

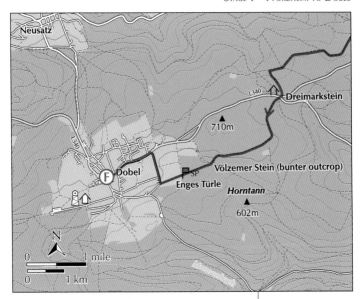

Großer Völzemer Stein

Straße to the left to the centre of the village at *Dobel/ Schulhaus* (school).

DOBEL

The small community of Dobel is situated on an open high plateau on the fringe of the Black Forest. It doesn't have much of a claim to fame, but it does have some fantastic views all the way to the Swabian Jura in the east, Odenwald in the northeast, Kraichgau to the north, the Palatinate Forest in the northwest and the Voges in the west. In the autumn, when the lower valleys are covered in a thick blanket of fog, Dobel is often still basking in the sun, an island in a sea of clouds.

Tourist information

Tourismusbüro Dobel: Neue Herrenalber Str. 11, 75335 Dobel, tel +49 (0)7083 74513, kontakt@dobel.info, **www.dobel.de/gaeste/tourist-information**

STAGE 2
Dobel to Forbach

Start	Schulhaus signpost, Dobel
Finish	Bahnhof Forbach signpost
Distance	25.6km
Ascent	590m
Descent	960m
Time	7hr
Refreshments	On Sat and Sun between April and October Hahnenfalzhütte serves drinks and snack food. Hotel and restaurant Sarbacher in Kaltenbronn (closed Mondays).

Once up on the Dobel plateau the trail runs relatively level to Kaltenbronn, either through the forest or along the edge of the hills, with far-ranging views. Although small by British standards, Kaltenbronn is Germany's largest coherent upland moor and one of the country's oldest nature reserves.

Nearby Hohlohturm offers fabulous views across the entire region. From here the trail descends, sometimes quite steeply, into the valley of the Murg. Take a break at Latschigfelsen – a conspicuous rocky promontory above the valley – to take in the views before descending to the picturesque town of Forbach, where the stage ends.

At *Dobel/Schulhaus* head straight on towards the *Kurhaus* (administrative centre) and pass through *Sonnentor Dobel* – the second Westweg portal.

> You might have noticed some peculiarly **painted benches** and other pieces of artwork scattered around the village. The benches were designed by different schools to represent the landmarks or national symbols of various countries.

By the 'Belgium bench' turn left up the hill towards the **observation tower** (open to the public between April

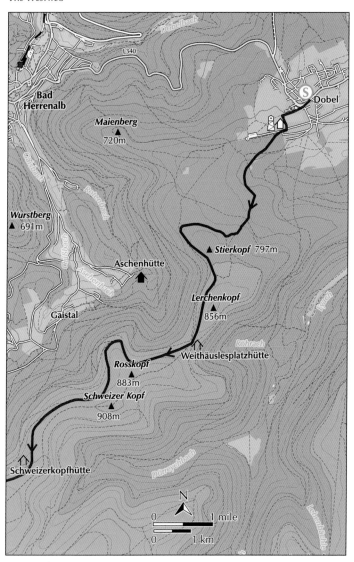

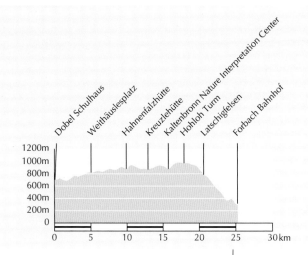

and October), pass the **walker's hostel** and turn right for about 150m to *Dobel/Aussichtsturm*, where Westweg branches off, half-left, into the forest.

After passing a couple of huts the trail reaches a trail crossing at *Pflanzengarten*. About 50m further along fork to the right onto a smaller track. At the T-junction turn right on the forest road. After about 1km watch out for the marker pointing to the left, where Westweg takes a shortcut via a small path that comes out at a fork of a forest road. Turn left onto the paved lane, then immediately take the left fork and continue on the forestry road (Althäuslesweg) to a picnic hut at **Weithäuslesplatz**.

Follow Hahnenfalzweg to the right of the hut. This is a great panoramic section with beautiful open views; the best places to admire them are the new 'sky benches' just before reaching **Schweizerkopfhütte**.

The open hillsides are not the result of clearcutting, as it may seem, but rather the aftermath of hurricane Lothar. There are many such areas, known as '**Sturmwurfflächen**', along the Westweg route,

Map continues on page 62

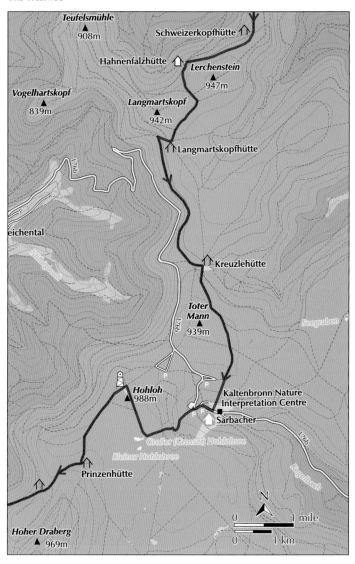

providing a small insight into the tremendous impact this storm has had on the region.

Continue straight on past an observation platform and keep to the left at the fork. At a bend, Westweg continues straight on, now on a smaller track that leads down to **Hahnenfalzhütte** – another prime picnic location high above Alb Valley.

Continue up the hill on the small track next to the one you came down on, which soon joins a forest road to the left (Ächtlersweg) and reaches a T-junction. Turn right to reach **Langmartskopfhütte**.

Pass the hut to the right and turn left at *Glasertwald* to follow the broad track to **Kreuzlehütte**. Turn right past the hut and keep to the right at the fork. At a bend, at *Schlagbaum*, follow the small path straight on to *Schlittenhang*, where Mittelweg rejoins Westweg for a short interlude and both head down to the **nature interpretation centre** by the road.

> **Kaltenbronner Hochmoor** is the largest protected upland moor in Germany. It originated at the end of the last glaciation, 10,000 years ago. Peat mosses and grasses thrived in the low temperature, high precipitation climate and covered the underlying Bunter sandstone. But as the layers of peat grew thicker the plants on the surface lost access to the mineral-rich bedrock, becoming entirely dependent on rainwater for their nutrients. Very few species can survive in such an extreme habitat; the ecosystem is thus populated with highly adapted plants and animals. Kaltenbronn was declared a nature reserve in 1940, making it one of the oldest protected areas in the country.

Turn right along the road, past the first car park. At the bend, by the second car park at *Kaltenbronn Parkplatz*, Westweg climbs up the hill next to a stream. Cross the dirt road and continue straight on at *Hohlohsee*. A boardwalk leads across an eerie moor that resembles a natural

Map continues on page 65

Walkway across Hohloh moor

art exhibit, with twisted roots – each a microcosm of its own – forming bizarre sculptures. At the other end follow the broad track to **Hohloh Turm**.

> **Hohloh Turm**, also known as Kaiser Wilhelm Turm, was one of the earliest observation towers built in the Black Forest. The first version, made of wood in the late 1850s, was replaced by a tower built with local sandstone boulders (Bunter) in 1897. But the surrounding trees kept on growing and thus an extension of a further 6.4m was added, bringing its total height to 28.6m. On clear days it is possible to see across the entire Black Forest – and with some squinting, even beyond Feldberg to the Alps, more than 200km away.

At *Hohloh Turm* head towards Prinzenhütte on the small trail to the left, which shortly afterwards joins a broad forestry road to the left and passes *Buchenloh*. At **Prinzenhütte** Westweg and Mittelweg part company.

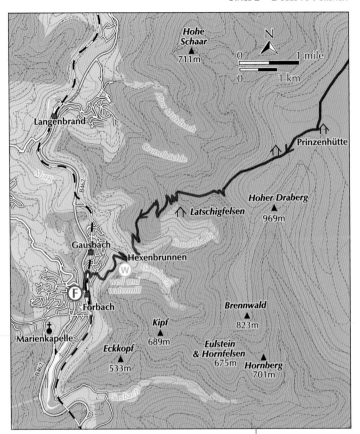

Westweg turns right and after approximately 1km reaches another hut. Follow the rough trail to the left of the hut down the hill, towards Latschigfelsen.

There are few markers here, but there are not many places where you can go wrong. At one point the trail bends to the left, but only to ease the gradient. Shortly afterwards it crosses another path. Continue straight on to reach **Latschigfelsen**.

Hut above Latschigfelsen

The rock promontory, 724m above the valley, allows for fabulous views of Murgtal. It has a little hut stuck on it, but just a little bit further down the trail there is another lookout point (Aussichtspunkt) without many human modifications.

From here the trails zigzags quite steeply down the hill. Shortly after *Ringberg*, join the broader forest road to the left, which comes to a T-junction. Turn right and watch out for an unexpected sharp turn to the left to follow a small, rather steep footpath directly down the hill. The trail emerges from the forest on a dirt road near a water fountain at **Hexenbrunnen**.

At *Hexenbrunnen* climb up to the lane above the water fountain and walk up the valley for a few metres. Take the farm track to the right passing fields and orchards. After about 800m turn right to reach the viewing platform at *Brückwaldanlage*. To the left of the platform a narrow little footpath leads down to **Gausbach**, coming out near the Westweg portal close to the train station. Bear left towards the river and left again to reach the **station** at *Bahnhof Forbach*.

Tyrolean huts of the Murg Valley

FORBACH

Like many other picturesque little towns that line the Murg Valley, Forbach made its fortunes from the once-flourishing timber and rafting trade. Today the town is rather sleepy. Its landmark is the covered wooden bridge across the Murg, which at 38.5m is one of the largest of its type in Europe. The characteristic little wooden huts that can be seen dotted around the fields were originally built by Tyrolean immigrants, who settled in the Murg Valley as forest workers some 250–300 years ago.

Tourist information

Tourist Information Forbach: Rathaus Forbach, Landstraße 27, 76596 Forbach, tel +40 (0)7228 390, touristinfo@forbach.de, **www.forbach.de**

Infozentrum Kaltenbronn: Kaltenbronn 600, 76593 Gernsbach-Kaltenbronn, tel +49 (0)7224 655 197, **www.infozentrum-kaltenbronn.de**

STAGE 3
Forbach to Unterstmatt

Start	Bahnhof Forbach
Finish	Unterstmatt ski area
Distance	19.6km
Ascent	1020m
Descent	380m
Time	6hr
Refreshments	Naturfreundehaus/Wanderheim Badener Höhe (closed Mondays), Bergwaldhütte am Sand (open Wednesday–Sunday), Hundseck Hundshütte (open Wednesday–Sunday in summer)

Although this stage is not that long, it is quite demanding. Several rather steep climbs add up to over 1000m that have to be overcome between Forbach and Unterstmatt. The day starts with a climb up to Wegscheidhütte (750m); the trail then heads down to Schwarzenbach-Talsperre (670m) – the largest water reservoir in the northern Black Forest – before continuing to climb, taking one peak after another: Badener Höhe (1002m), Hundseck (856m) and Hochkopf (1038m), and finally reaching Unterstmatt (928m) at the end of the day.

Walk past the station at **Forbach** and cross the covered wooden bridge. Cross Landstraße and head up the hill. After passing *Mosesbrunnen* fork to the left and follow Marienstraße to **Marienkapelle** – a chapel overlooking Forbach.

Just after the chapel the trail enters the forest, forks to the right and heads up the valley along the edge of the forest, following a little stream. Halfway up the valley, the trail takes an unexpected left turn and starts climbing up the hill. The route alternates between steep, narrow zigzag paths and short sections of forest road

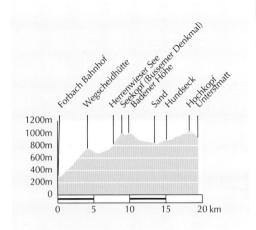

and eventually reaches **Wegscheidhütte** – a shelter hut by a huge trail junction.

Covered wooden bridge in Forbach

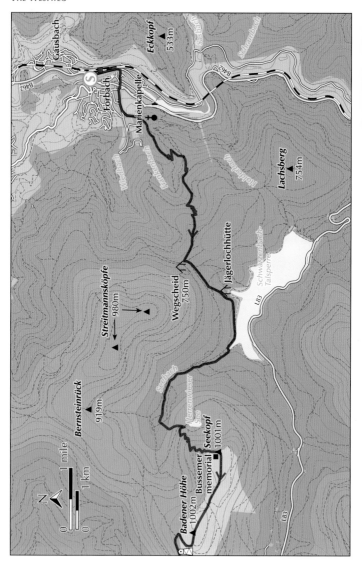

Pass the hut and follow the broad forest road to the left, towards Seeufer. At a tight bend Westweg branches off to the left and passes **Jägerlochhütte** above the **Schwarzenbachtal reservoir** on the way down to *Stauseeufer*. Continue along the shore to the right to reach *Seebachmündung*, where Seebach (stream) enters the reservoir.

Map continues on page 73

Cross the stream and turn right to follow Seebach up the valley. After passing *Seebachbrücke*, just before a bend, Westweg branches to the left and heads up to **Herrenwieser See** via a stony track.

> **Herrenwieser See** is a serene spot just off the main trail. To find it, simply follow the yellow marker at the Herrenwieser See signpost. This is a good place for a picnic before starting the rather steep ascent to Badener Höhe.

Cross the forest road at *Herrenwieser See* and continue on the other side, where the trail almost immediately branches off the broad track and starts to zigzag up the headwall on a steep and rocky path to **Seekopf** (1001m), by a memorial stone.

> The memorial, known as **Bussemer Stein**, commemorates Philipp Bussemer (1855–1918), one of the founding fathers of the Schwarzwaldverein and initiator of the first long-distance routes through the Black Forest.

Turn right at *Seekopf/Bussemer Stein* and head for **Badener Höhe** (1002m), with its historic tower, Friedrichsturm. ▸ Follow the broad forest road down to **Herrenwieser Sattel** and turn left to a second signpost, also called *Herrenwieser Sattel*, where Westweg forks to the right to take a shortcut through the forest. ▸

Dating back to 1890, Friedrichsturm was among the first observation towers constructed by the Schwarzwaldverein.

After rejoining the gravel road the trail passes Naturfreundehaus Badener Höhe and café/guesthouse Bergwaldhütte am Sand, before emerging from the forest by the spooky looking Sand Hotel, right by the B500 road.

The area around Herrenwieser Sattel forms part of the new National Park Schwarzwald.

Friedrichsturm at Badener Höhe

The trail crosses the B500 in two places: at Sand, and at Hundseck. The B500 – or **Schwarzwaldhochstraße** – was Germany's first 'touring' road in the days when cars were still a novelty. Some rather pompous hotels that were built along that road once attracted glamorous clientele, but their days of glory have long since faded and they are now quite dilapidated and lost in time.

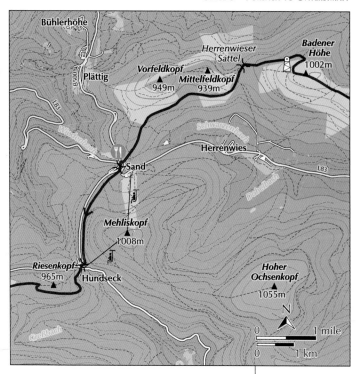

Head for the big road junction (B500/L83) to *Sand/Kapelle*. Follow the broad track to the left, which runs parallel to the B500 past *Schwarzbergle* to the ski area at **Hundseck**. Cross the car park and the road and follow the forest track to the left of *Hundseck Hotel*. Just after passing *Hundseck Sprungschanze*, fork to the right and head up the hill. By the timber landing look for a smaller trail to the right that leads up into the forest. ▶

Keep to the left to reach *Hinterm Riesenköpfle*, then join the old gravel track to the right, around the edge of the hill, with views back towards Hundseck and Badener Höhe. After passing some picnic benches the trail reaches a big sign that reads 'Schonwald

Timber landings are forest clearings, often at trail junctions, where logs are stored before they are transported to the sawmill.

Map continues on page 74

73

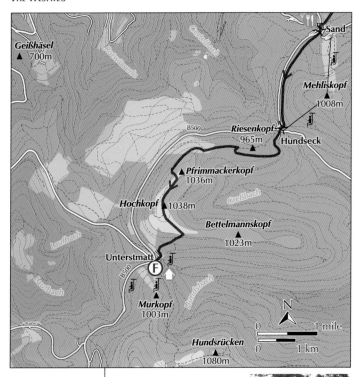

Sheep, employed as lawnmowers, on Hochkopf

Hochkopf-Pfrimmackerkopf'. Follow the small path up the hill to the upland moor of Hochkopf.

Walk straight across the top of **Hochkopf** (1038m), which is marked by a concrete bench, and down the other side where the trail arrives on a dirt road just above Unterstmatt car park. Turn left and head down towards the road and car park at **Unterstmatt ski area**.

UNTERSTMATT

Unterstmatt is just a little ski area, busy during the winter and dead in the summer. But the sunset views across the Rhine Valley over to Strasbourg and the Vosges are hard to beat. There are a couple of simple and convenient little hotels here.

Tourist information

Bühl: Hauptstraße 47, 77815 Bühl, tel +49 (0)7223 935332, tourist.info@buehl. de, **www.buehl.de**

Bühlertal: Hauptstr. 92, 77830 Bühlertal, tel +49 (0)7223 99670, tourist.info@ buehlertal.de, **www.buehlertal.de**

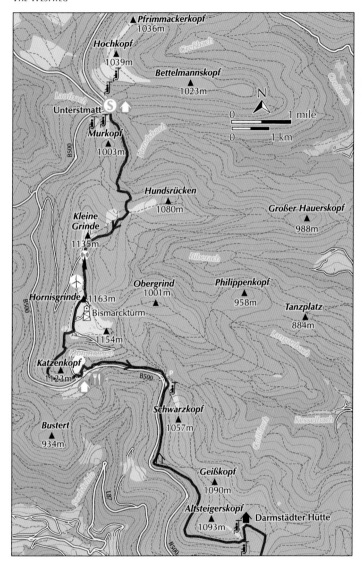

STAGE 4

Unterstmatt to Alexanderschanze

Start	Unterstmatt ski area
Finish	Alexanderschanze
Distance	27.8km
Ascent	700m
Descent	650m
Time	8hr
Refreshments	Ochsenstall, Mummelsee, Seibels-Eckle, Darmstädter Hütte, Ruhestein Schänke, Grenzstüble (closed Monday–Thursday), Schliffkopf Hotel, Zuflucht
Note	It's best to walk this section during the week as it is often busy on weekends and noise from roaring motorbikes that are touring the B500 can be annoying.

The fourth stage gets top marks for grand vistas, but it's a long day's hike. After a steep ascent to Hornisgrinde (1163m), the highest peak of the northern Black Forest, the trail passes a rather tacky tourist trap at Mummelsee. But once that's left behind the route becomes quite delightful as it climbs up to the central spine of the Black Forest massif. Due to the effects of hurricane Lothar there are fabulous, unobstructed views for much of the way. The trail crosses the B500 near Ruhestein, where the headquarters and nature interpretation centre of the National Park are located. From here it climbs up to Schliffkopf, an open mountaintop with far ranging views, which remain unobstructed for much of the way to Alexanderschanze, where this stage ends.

At **Unterstmatt** cross the car park and head for the ski-lift across the road, then follow the path to the left of the cashier hut into the forest. After crossing a little bridge, cross a forest road and continue straight on, further up the hill. After crossing a second small bridge briefly join a forest road to the left and then fork to the right, towards Ski- und Wanderheim Ochsenstall.

Map continues on page 81

The trail up to Hornisgrinde

The trail meets another forest road and joins it to the left. By the hostel turn right on the track that leads up to a barrier. Here Westweg branches to the right and climbs steeply up the hill on a small path. Near the top bear left past a shelter hut and the huge TV mast. Keep to the left and pass the wind turbines at *Hornisgrinde/Windpark* to reach **Hornisgrinde** (1163m).

> **Hornisgrinde**, the highest mountain of the northern Black Forest, has a distinctly odd atmosphere – almost like an abandoned post-industrial site – especially around Hornisgrinde Turm. In the light of its history, this is unsurprising. Prior to WWII Hornisgrinde was a popular tourist spot, but in 1942 the Nazis took it over and turned it into an airbase. In 1945, after the liberation, the French army occupied the hill and used it as a radio transmission base for its secret service until the end of the Cold War. But the site was only officially released in 1997 and the task of managing it was handed over to local communities.

Great efforts have been made to restore the degraded upland moor, but the scars are still very evident. To intensify the rehabilitation efforts Hornisgrinde has been declared a nature reserve. Boardwalks have been laid across the bog and picking herbs or berries is prohibited.

Follow the trail along the edge of the hilltop to the observation tower at *Hornisgrinde/Bismarckturm*, then bear right and head towards *Beim Hornisgrindeturm* (1158m). Here Westweg turns off to the right to follow a small path down the hill, past *Bergwachthütte* and *Katzenkopf*, to reach **Berghotel Mummelsee**.

Pass in front of the hotel and continue along the lake past the playground. After about 50m the trail forks to the right, heading towards the modernistic chapel at *Mummelseekapelle*, right by the Westweg portal. From here a track runs down the hill, parallel to the road past *Mummelseewald* to *Seibelseckle* car park.

Ex-military Hornisgrinde tower

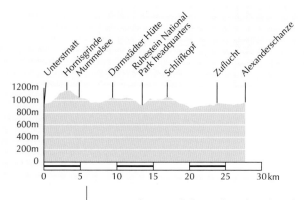

Cross the car park diagonally to the right and continue next to the ski-lift, past the barrier on the broad forest road.

ROUTE NOTE

There are currently negotiations underway to change the routing for this section of Westweg. The alternative route would join 'Seensteig' and climb up the hill next to Seibelseckle-Skilift. This route follows a smaller path that runs a bit higher up over to Skilift/Darmstädter Hütte, where it would continue as described below. In bad weather conditions the broad track is the better option, but otherwise this small path is the more interesting route.

The broad track skirts the edge of **Schwarzkopf** to reach a picnic hut and then continues on the right-hand fork, on Hellmut-Gnädinger-Weg. After 200m Westweg takes the left fork to the Lothar monument.

Continue straight on to *Skilift/Darmstädter Hütte*, and then turn left, towards the serviced hut **Darmstädter Hütte**. Pass in front of the hut to the right and follow the boardwalk across the bog to *Bannwald*. Briefly turn right before forking off onto a smaller path to the left.

After rejoining the broader track and passing *Eutinger Denkmal* (memorial) the trail reaches the ski-lift and heads down to **Ruhestein**, where the headquarter of the national park is located.

Map continues on page 84

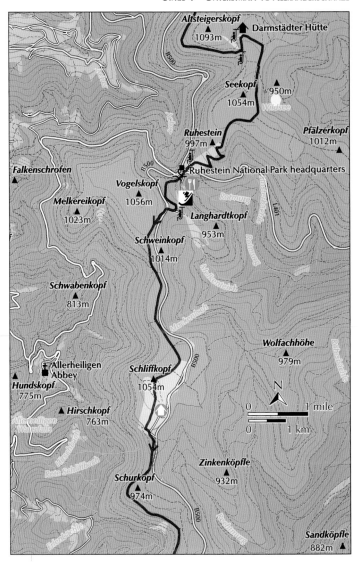

Eutinger memorial marks the grave of **Dr Euting** (1839–1913), a German orientalist with a special love for the Black Forest and the Vosges. He was a founding member of the Vosges Club and among the first to promote both of these mountain ranges as walking destinations.

Cross the road towards *Ruhestein Parkplatz* (car park) and follow the gravel track up the hill for about 50m, then branch to the right on a rougher trail towards the ski jumping ramp. At the top cross the car park and the road (B500) and continue on the track opposite across another patch of moor.

The trail merges with a bigger track to the left and reaches a trail junction at *Schweinkopf*. Take the left fork to the bend and then follow the smaller path straight on, passing *Hübscher Platz* on the way to **Schliffkopf** (1054m).

Schliffkopf – the best vantage point along the northern spine of the massif

The **open space** around Schliffkopf provides fabulous 360° views. This area is part of the national park and is subject to strict nature protection laws, so please stay on the trails. This is a precious wildlife habitat for wood grouse, grass snakes and the European adder.

Panoramic trail from Schliffkopf to Zuflucht

After enjoying the views, continue straight past Rechtmurgkopf and head down to *Steinmäuerle*. Bear left to *Steinmäuerle Infotafel* (information board). Here briefly take the trail to the right, which runs parallel to the road. At the trail crossing turn right and follow the very scenic track straight on, past *Schwabenrank*. At *Haferrütterank* take the left fork to reach **Lotharpfad**.

Just to the left, a trail (Lotharpfad) runs through an area that has been left pretty much as it was after **hurricane Lothar** swept through in 1999. It is

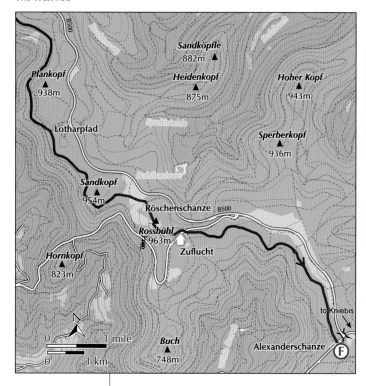

fascinating not only to see the root sculptures left by the dead trees, but also to appreciate the processes of natural regeneration.

After skirting around **Sandkopf** the panoramic trail comes to an end. Westweg reaches a paved path and joins it to the right. At a bend, Westweg briefly continues straight on before turning right and starting to climb steeply up to the ski-lift at Zuflucht. At the top bear left to **Röschenschanze**.

Construction of these **defence earthworks** started in 1794 and was meant to protect Württemberg's borders. However, Napoleon seized it in 1796 before construction was complete. Today nature has conquered it and it has been declared a nature reserve. Please do not enter.

Just before the car park keep to the left and head towards the road and another parking area.

At *Zuflucht Parkplatz* turn left, and at the end of the bus stop cross the road to follow a small paved trail into the forest to *Zuflucht*. At the fork, take the gravel path to the right to *Bei der Zollstockhütte*. Continue to the left, parallel to the road, to reach *Badberg* and **Alexanderschanze**.

ALEXANDERSCHANZE

There are many *Schanzen* (trenches) along the central ridge of the Black Forest, as it has often been the main defence line between various warring factions, particularly in the 17th and 18th centuries and mostly against the French.

Alexanderschanze is the end of this stage, but the best option for accommodation is the hostel at Zuflucht. If Zuflucht is fully booked look for alternatives in Kniebis. Some hotels in Kniebis offer a pick-up service for Westweg walkers and will also return you to the trail the next day – a great service well worth using, considering the length of this day's walk. Moreover, the last bit to Kniebis seems far longer than what the sign says, and if you arrive late you may miss dinner, as kitchens close at 8pm.

Tourist information

Besucherzentrum Schwarzwaldhochstraße: Freudenstadt-Kniebis, 72250 Freudenstadt, touristinfo@kniebis.de, **www.kniebis.de**

Nationalparkzentrum Ruhestein: Schwarzwaldhochstr. 2, 77889 Seebach, **www.schwarzwald-nationalpark.de**

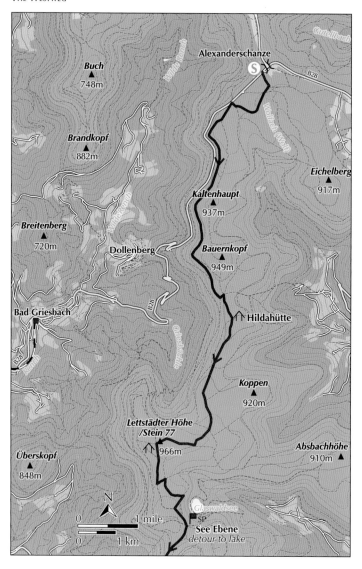

Alexanderschanze

Buch
748m

B28

Brandkopf
882m

Eichelberg
917m ▲

Kaltenhaupt
937m ▲

Breitenberg
720m ▲

Dollenberg

Bauernkopf
949m ▲

Bad Griesbach

↑↑ Hildahütte

B28

Koppen
920m ▲

*Lettstädter Höhe
/Stein 77*

Überskopf
848m ▲

↑↑
966m

Absbachhöhe
910m ▲

N

0 _____ 1 mile
0 _____ 1 km

Glaswaldsee

■ SP

See Ebene
detour to lake

STAGE 5

Alexanderschanze to Hark

Start	Alexanderschanze
Finish	Harkhof guesthouse, Hark
Distance	17.1km
Ascent	290m
Descent	550m
Time	5hr
Refreshments	None

This stage is relatively short and easy, without too many up and downs. Much of the way runs through the forest on broad forestry tracks, with occasional open views. The trail passes Hildahütte and Lettstädter Höhe (966m) on its way to Glaswaldsee – another tarn lying hidden among the firs. (Westweg does not go directly to the lake, but a detour is signposted from See Ebene.)

Keep a close eye on the markers as the route frequently switches between forest tracks and smaller trails. After Littweger Höhe the trail runs along the eastern side of the ridge to Hark – an isolated and rustic but cosy guesthouse snuggled into the fold of a valley.

At **Alexanderschanze** look for the big boulder marked 'Dreifürstenstein' by the side of the road, and follow the small path into the woods.

Map continues on page 89

> **Dreifürstenstein** is an old boundary stone that marked the border between the kingdom of Württemberg, the bishopric of Strasbourg and the county of Fürstenberg (later Baden). The historic boundary stone is not the boulder, but a small stone located a few metres down the trail.

Pass the boundary stone and *Wolfursprung* and continue straight. ▶ By the broad forest road at

Ignore the pointer to the left towards Westweg-Portal in Kniebis, unless you really want to get your stamp – it's 1.8km away from the trail.

An area of forest affected by Hurricane Lothar

Don't be confused by the red and yellow markers on the tree stump; they refer to local trails.

Wolfursprung/Grenzweg, cross diagonally to the right and continue straight, on Schanzenweg. At the end briefly join Heuplatzweg to the right to reach a lay-by at *Neuer Höhenweg.* ◄

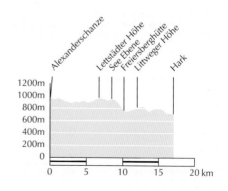

The trail continues parallel to the road through the forest. After passing *Heuplatz* it reaches a clearing on the edge of the hill, which is used as a jump-off point for paragliders and offers lovely views of Renchtal.

At *Graseck* briefly turn left, and after about 70m turn right to reach *Hildahütte*. Take the small trail straight on, past *Schnepfenmoos*, to get to another shelter hut at **Lettstädter Höhe/Stein77**. Here Westweg turns left, down the hill through fairly open terrain. At the next crossing, by some big boulders, briefly turn left and then right onto a forestry road.

Turn right at *Seeblick* and climb up the hill again on a smaller path. Keep to the left and at a T-junction turn left to the big trail junction at *See Ebene*. Continue straight for about 80m, then fork to the right. The trail merges with a forestry road to the right and heads straight down the hill on Stegerlesweg, past *Am Klagstein* and

Map continues on page 90

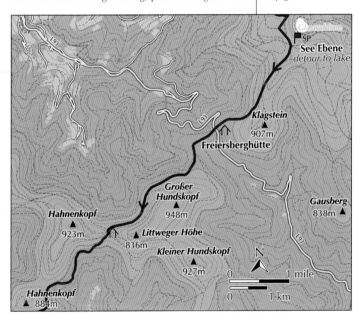

89

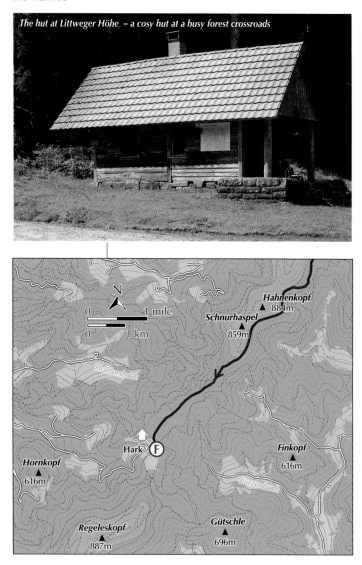

The hut at Littweger Höhe – a cosy hut at a busy forest crossroads

Juliusbrunnen. At the bottom it reaches a **shelter hut** at *Freiersberg*, right by a road (L93). ▶

Cross the road and follow the broad track straight on, up the hill on Hundskopfsträßle, past *Am Hundskopf* to a big trail junction and shelter hut at **Littweger Höhe**. Cross the junction and continue half-left, past the hut and down the hill on a broad track. Watch out for the markers; after about 50m Westweg branches off to the left, on a smaller footpath that is easily missed!

The trail reaches a forestry road and joins it to the right. After about 500m Westweg again branches off to the right and climbs up the hill. At the top join the forestry road to the left and bear right on Herbensattelweg by the timber landing. At the fork bear left. The path again meets with a forestry road and continues to the left to *Jägerbrünnele*. Just before the trail reaches the edge of the forest, fork to the left to reach **Hark**. Harkhof guesthouse is the farm right below.

The Westweg portal 'Freiersberger Tor' does not mark the end of this stage.

HARK

Hark is no more than an isolated farmhouse/guesthouse, but a very beautiful and authentic spot to end the day. If Harkhof is fully booked, hotels and B&Bs in Oberharmersbach are the best alternative. Many hotels offer a pick-up/drop-off service for Westweg walkers. If you prefer to walk, follow the blue marker to Oberharmersbach (5km), but be aware that the town stretches up through the valley for 12km! There is also a walkers' hostel at Brandenkopf (route described in the next stage), or, if you're really ambitious, you can walk all the way to Hausach (the total distance from Alexanderschanze to Hausach is 32km!).

Tourist information

Oberharmersbach: Dorf 60, 77784 Oberharmersbach, tel +49 (0)7837 277, tourist-info@oberharmersbach.net, **www.oberharmersbach.de**

STAGE 6
Hark to Hausach

Start	Harkhof guesthouse, Hark
Finish	Hausach/Wintergarten signpost, Hausach
Distance	16km; via Brandenkopf: 21km
Ascent	320m; via Brandenkopf: 375m
Descent	780m; via Brandenkopf: 835m
Time	5hr; via Brandenkopf: 6hr
Refreshments	Wanderheim Brandenkopf (open 10am–8pm except Mondays), Hohenlochenhütte (only weekends and public holidays), Café/Restaurant Käppelehof (closed Mondays and Tuesdays, except on public holidays).

Like the previous stage, this one runs mostly through the forest. The day's highlight is Hohenlochenhütte, which easily rates as the cutest hut in the entire Black Forest. It is usually closed, but during the walking season volunteers serve homemade cake and coffee on weekends and public holidays. It is well worth a stop for its fabulous views, even when closed. The other highlight is Spitzfelsen – a rocky outcrop above Kinzigtal – which comes just before the start of the steep descent to Hausach.

At Am Reiherskopf, Westweg splits into two variants. One branch leads up to Brandenkopf (945m), while the other traverses the eastern slope of Reiherskopf down to Hirzwasen, where the two branches merge again. There's a Schwarzwaldverein guesthouse and an observation tower on Brandenkopf, but the hilltop itself is covered in trees and only the tower offers any interesting views.

From **Hark** take the field track along the edge of the valley to Harkhöhe. Continue to the left for about 50m to Bei St Gallus, then fork to the right. Cross a forestry road and climb up through the forest on a small path to reach a trail junction. Turn left for about 100m, then branch to the right, up the hill.

Map continues on page 98

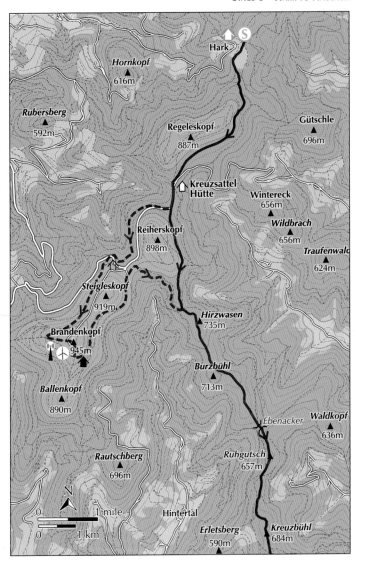

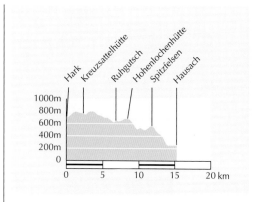

The trail meets a forestry road and joins it to the left, and after about 1.5km it reaches **Kreuzsattelhütte**. Cross the trail junction and follow the paved lane to the right to *Am Reiherskopf*, where you have the option of taking a detour via Brandenkopf (see below).

For the main route, fork onto the stony track, which climbs slightly, skirts around Reiherskopf and then comes down to Hirzwasen, where the two trails meet again.

Brandenkopf variant

At *Am Reiherskopf* continue on the paved lane for about 100m, then fork off onto the forestry road to the right and keep walking straight until the trail comes to a little road, where Gründlesweg crosses Steiglesweg, by a **shelter hut**. Cross the road and pass the hut on the gravel track heading up the hill.

At *Spitzbrunnen*, Westweg meets another forestry road at a bend and continues uphill to the left, together with Hansjakobweg (hat symbol).

Heinrich Hansjakob was a country vicar and author of popular fiction, who based his stories on the local history, people and places of the Black Forest – many of which are commemorated along the 'große und kleine Hansjakobweg'.

Brandenkopf Turm

Just before the wind turbine the trail branches to the left onto a smaller path. At *Farnlehenkopf* turn left towards the guesthouse and observation tower at **Brandenkopf** (945m).

Brandenkopf lies roughly at the centre of the Black Forest and from the observation tower the sweeping views encompass the whole region. Regrettably, neither the TV transmitter opposite the guesthouse nor the nearby wind turbines enhance the ambience of this place.

Walk past the guesthouse and take the small trail next to the TV transmitter to the right, down to *Oberer Brandenkopfweg*. Turn left and follow the right-hand fork, down the hill to a T-junction. At *Am Steigleskopf* choose the gravel track to the left, to *Bettelfrau*, where the trail joins another forest road at a bend. Bear right on Hirzwasenweg. At a bend just past Alt-Wolfacherkopfweg, fork to the right onto the small trail, which leads to a big trail junction, where the two routes reunite at **Hirzwasen**.

Pass the crucifix to the right. By a milestone in the middle of the forest, the trail forks to the left, to *Schmieders Höhe*. Here take the right-hand fork down to a clearing at *Ebenacker*, by a paved lane. The trail passes the clearing to the left and continues straight on and past a second signpost, also called *Ebenacker*. It reaches a T-junction and joins the forestry road to the left, to a crossroads.

Bear left to continue more or less straight on, now on a smaller track, past Bergbauernhöhe to a crossing by a sign for Eckhardsbrunnen Quelle. Keep to the right, towards Hohenlochenhütte. Shortly afterwards, at a bend, Westweg branches off to the left on a very small path. Keep going straight, and by the sign for Ehemalige

Hohenlochenhütte, above Kinzig Valley; easily the cutest hut in the Black Forest

Gayerhütte Aussichtspunkt (viewpoint), bear right on the small path to reach **Hohenlochenhütte**.

After enjoying the views, continue on the trail, which soon turns into a narrow path that runs along the edge of the hill. Ignore all the little paths branching to the left. Eventually the trail merges with a broader track and continues down the hill. This track in turn runs into a forestry road and turns right, to a T-junction at *Osterbachsattel* and then turns left. The trail emerges from the forest and branches to the right, to another signpost, also called *Osterbachsattel*. ▶

Here Westweg turns left and re-enters the forest. The path crosses the forestry road again and continues on a smaller trail to *Am Bildstock*. Turn left to *Weißes Kreuz*. Pass the crucifix and picnic table and head down the hill towards a pasture. Walk along the edge of the field to *Dohlenbacherhöhe*, where Westweg and Hansjakobweg part company.

Käppelehof, just off the trail

To the right lies Café/Restaurant Käppelehof (closed Mondays and Tuesdays, except on public holidays).

Spitzfelsen

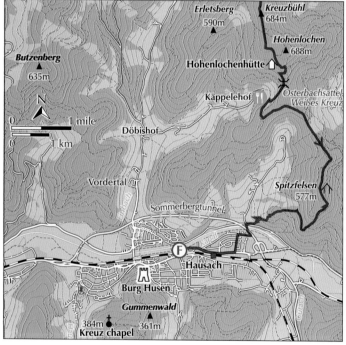

Walk straight on, steeply up the hill. At the top, turn right to reach a trail crossing at *Hofberg*. Take the left fork, past the antenna, to **Spitzfelsen** – a rocky outcrop with a little shelter hut and nice views of the Kinzig valley.

From here the trail runs straight down the hill on a small, steep and stony path through the forest, crossing a lane along the way. At the bottom turn right along the lane to a T-junction at *Hochbehälter/Kleine Kinzig* (water reservoir; 457m). Turn right and at the bend branch off to the left to continue on a small trail until it reaches a gravel track.

Follow the bend to the right and look for a small path forking to the left, which runs below the level of the gravel track. Soon it reaches a field track by a bench and turns left. Just before the track re-enters the forest, take the small, steep path down to *Frohnaustraße*, and cross the wooden footbridge over the **River Kinzig**.

On the other side pass the soccer field. The trail runs underneath the big bridge and then turns right on Inselstraße. At the first crossing turn left on Römerstraße

View from Spitzfelsen across the Kinzig valley

to the T-junction at *Hausach/Blume*. Turn right on Eisenbahnstraße and head towards the station and the centre of town. (Alternatively you could walk along the River Kinzig, or follow Inselstraße straight on, until it crosses Eisenbahnstraße by the church.)

After passing the church, Eisenbahnstraße turns into Hauptstraße and reaches the Westweg portal at *Hausach/Wintergarten* (**Hausach**).

HAUSACH

The River Kinzig represents a major east-west artery through the Black Forest, which the Romans were the first to develop as a route for moving troops between the Rhine and Neckar rivers. Hausach is one of the pretty little towns that line the Kinzig valley. It lies at the lowest point of altitude along the Westweg route.

Tourist information

Tourist Information Hausach: Hauptstr. 40, 77756 Hausach, tel +49 (0)7831 7975, tourist-info@hausach.de, **www.hausach.de**

HAUSACH TO TITISEE

Burg Husen (Hausach) (Stage 7)

STAGE 7
Hausach to Wilhelmshöhe

Start	Hausach/Wintergarten signpost, Hausach
Finish	Wilhelmshöhe guesthouse (restaurant closed Wednesdays and Thursdays)
Distance	20.2km
Ascent	1135m
Descent	400m
Time	6hr 30min
Refreshments	Hotel-restaurant Schöne Aussicht at Karlstein; Haus Silberberg

From the bottom of the deeply incised Kinzig valley, the trail ascends steeply up to Farrenkopf (789m) and continues along the central spine of the Black Forest, sometimes down but mostly up, overcoming more than 1000m of altitude gain along the way. Due to its strategic location, this area has borne the brunt of many a conflict throughout history – especially with neighbouring France. Numerous trenches, buried in the countryside, bear silent witness to this troubled past. Today they provide resting spots from which to admire the far-ranging views. Two rocky outcrops – Huberfelsen and Karlstein – also make scenic lookout points.

The end of the stage is at Wilhelmshöhe, a rustic guesthouse right on the route and close to Schonach and Triberg – the rival hotspots of cuckoo-clock manufacturing.

From *Hausach/Wintergarten* (**Hausach**), by the Westweg portal, take the steps down to the road and pass under the railway bridge. Follow the main road (Hauptstraße) through town. At the corner of Kreuzbergstraße briefly turn left, and by the old water fountain at *Hausach/ Aufgang Schloßberg* take the footpath on the left up to the old castle ruin of **Burg Husen**.

Burg Husen, above Hausach, Kinzig Valley

Burg Husen was built during the 13th century to protect nearby silver mines. It fell victim to the savage frenzy of destruction during the Thirty Years' War (1618–1648).

The trail continues behind the castle. Follow the gravel track up the hill and ignore the log ladder. At *Oberhalb Burg Husen* join the forestry road to the left and follow it around the bend.

Cross Sägebeckweg and continue steeply up the hill on the small zigzag path. At the top join a bigger track to the right. By a timber landing cross the forestry road and follow the small trail opposite, which eventually reaches a gravel road. Briefly bear left, then right, following the gravel road out of the forest to *Überm Fuggishof*. Just past

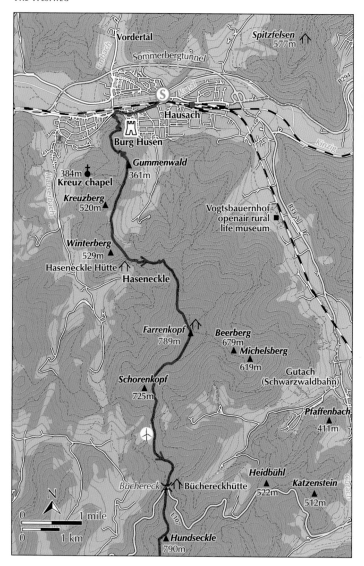

the signpost take the small path to the left, through the forest to **Haseneckle Hütte**.

The path levels out for a short respite and continues straight on to *Haseneckle*, where it meets a forest road. But instead of joining it, Westweg takes a smaller track to the left of the road. This last section (2km) up to Farrenkopf is really steep. By a kind of old tree chute turn right for about 30m, then join a bigger track to the left. After passing an insect hotel, the trail splits, and confusingly there are Westweg markers on both trails. Choose either one; they both come out at the same place. Pass a bench with a pair of boots nailed to it. ▸

The inscription reads: 'You have only truly experienced the places that you have explored on foot'.

Join the gravel road to the right, and about 20m after *Zinowald* take the smaller track, half right, further up the hill. After crossing another gravel road, the trail suddenly bends to the left in the middle of the forest before finally reaching **Farrenkopf** (789m) with its comfortable shelter hut and grill area – a good place to a take a well-deserved break and enjoy the beautiful views.

On the other side of the hut the trail runs quite steeply down the hill to a forest road. Cross slightly to the left and take the small, fairly level path through the woods. (Not very obvious!) The trail meets a gravel road and briefly joins it to the left. At a bend, watch out for a small trail on the left that runs along the edge of the hill.

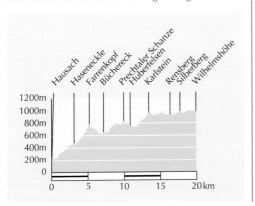

Map continues on page 106

105

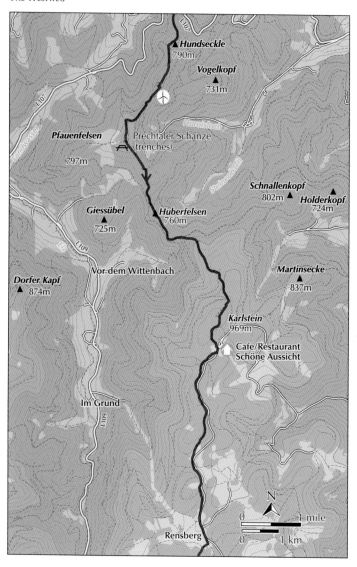

At the T-junction briefly turn right, then follow the track to the left down the hill on a small stony trail to *Am Schorenkopf*. Continue half-left towards the wind park access road. After passing the wind turbine, fork off onto a forest track to the left to reach a **picnic hut** at *Büchereck*. Pass the hut and cross the barrier heading towards the road at *Büchereck Parkplatz*.

Cross the road and briefly follow Bücherneckweg. After about 30m, Westweg branches off onto a steep and stony path that leads straight up the hill. After about 500m fork to the right. The path begins to level out and reaches a T-junction by a timber landing. Turn left, and just before the wind turbine turn off onto the old forestry track to the right.

Just before a bend the trail unexpectedly branches to the left onto a small footpath to climb up the hill to reach a walled enclosure. There are no signs to explain the structure but it seems to be a redout. Walk along the wall to the right, and in the corner take the steep zigzag path down through the trees. The trail is a bit unclear, but some pink spray paint markings on the trees help to indicate the way.

At the bottom turn left for about 10m, then turn right onto a smaller path to the right. The trail meets a broader track and joins it to the left, towards the wind park access road. Just before reaching the road turn right and follow the small path through the forest. By the T-junction turn right on the old forestry road.

After about 100m, by an old water fountain and an unnamed signpost, Westweg turns up the hill to the left on a small zigzag trail and is joined by Querweg Lahr-Rottweil. At the top turn right onto the forestry road. Just after passing another wind turbine the trail forks; stay on the broad track to the right and continue straight on to **Prechtaler Schanze**, where a picnic table offers good views of Elztal and the surrounding mountains. ▶

The Zweitälersteig joins Westweg here.

Just after the picnic table the trail turns off to the right and passes through some more recent trenches – stark reminders of a more belligerent age. Follow the steep path down the hill.

Map continues on page 109

Huberfelsen

At the bottom turn right and follow the broader forest road to a trail junction at **Huberfelsen**. Briefly turn left, and after about 20m fork off onto the small path through the bushes on the right.

Huberfelsen rock juts out like a rhino-horn. There are roughly hewn steps that lead to the top, which is secured by a fence. The rock is named to honour a local steward (1810) who was well respected for his service to the poor peasants.

Just below Huberfelsen a perfectly placed bench overlooks Prechtal, Elztal and the Vosges on the distant horizon. Follow the trail around the rock and rejoin the forest road by another picnic bench. Turn right to *Hirzdobel*, where Zweitälersteig and Westweg part company. After about 200m, just before running into another track at a bend, Westweg branches off onto a smaller path to the left. Shortly afterwards, Westweg and Querweg Lahr-Rottweil separate and Westweg forks to the right, to start climbing up towards Karlstein. At the top the trail passes a bench and continues to the right, up the hill. The trail meets another forestry track at a bend and joins it to the left.

Keep climbing up the hill. Eventually the trail bends to the left and meets another track, which it joins to the left for only about 20m before forking to the left onto a smaller path again for the final steep ascent to **Karlstein**. This turn can easily be missed!

Karlstein, a rocky outcrop with nice views to the east and south, is named after Carl Eugene of Württemberg – a Duke with megalomaniac tendencies, whose extravaganzas and ambitions for riches and glory nearly ruined his duchy and imposed severe hardships on its people. He is said to have visited the rock in 1770.

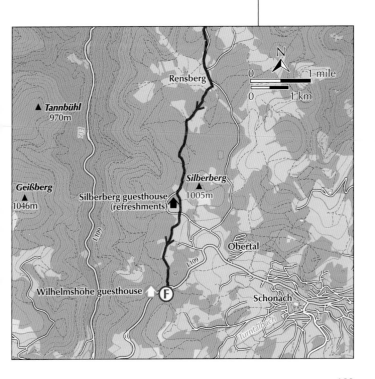

From here a rocky trail leads down the hill and joins a forest track to the left. Head towards the road. On the opposite side of the road is hotel-restaurant **Schöne Aussicht**, which not only offers lovely views but also some mean cake!

Cross the car park, past signpost *Hauenstein* and head back into the forest behind the playing field. At *Vogelloch* join another forestry track to the right. The trail runs pretty much parallel to the road. After passing *Absetze* keep to the left to a country lane. Continue straight past Gasthaus **Rensberg**, where the lane meets a slightly bigger back-road. Just before the bend fork to the right, onto a field track. Pass *Erwin Schweitzer Heim* and turn right by the building, past the fire pond, uphill. Pass the old gate on the left – all that remains of Herrenwälder Hof, which after it was sold was moved, lock, stock and barrel, to another location.

Haus Silberberg – a little B&B just before Wilhelmshöhe

Keep to the left, and just past **Vesperstube Haus Silberberg** follow the field track to the left up the hill, past *Gummelekreuz* and straight on Lukas Kuner Weg to **Wilhelmshöhe**.

WILHELMSHÖHE, SCHONACH/TRIBERG

The Wilhelmshöhe guesthouse lies just outside Schonach – one of the traditional strongholds of cuckoo clock production. If cuckoo clocks are your thing you can visit the second largest cuckoo clock in the world, with a clockwork measuring 3.60m x 3.10m, in Schonach. (An even bigger one can be seen a little bit further away, at Eble Uhren-Park in Triberg.)

Triberg, just up the road, is 'Kitsch Central' of the Black Forest, making all other such outposts seem like harmless renditions thereof. Apart from cuckoo clocks, woodcarvings and a museum that celebrates quintessential Black Forest traditions, its major claim to fame is its waterfall, which is the highest in Germany outside the Alps.

Also nearby and worth a visit is the open-air museum Vogtsbauernhof, which provides a rich insight into the hard everyday life of the rural population in the not-too-distant past.

Cuckoo clocks

Walk-in Cuckoo-Clock: Untertalstraße 28, 78136 Schonach im Schwarzwald, tel +49 (0)7722 4689

Eble Uhrenpark: Schonachbach 27, 78098 Triberg im Schwarzwald, tel +49 (0)7722 96220, info@eble-uhren-park.de

Museums

Schwarzwaldmuseum Triberg: Wallfahrtstraße 4, 78098 Triberg, tel +49 (0)7722 4434, **www.schwarzwaldmuseum.de**

Open-air Museum Vogtsbauernhof: 77793 Gutach (Schwarzwaldbahn), tel +49 (0)7831 93560, info@vogtsbauernhof.de, **www.vogtsbauernhof.de**

Tourist information

Tourist Information Schonach: Haus des Gastes, Hauptstraße 6, 78136 Schonach im Schwarzwald, tel +49 (0)7722 964810, info@schonach.de, **www.schonach.de**

Tourist-Info Triberg: Wallfahrtstraße 4, 78098 Triberg im Schwarzwald, tel +49 (0)7722 866490, tourist-info@triberg.net, **www.triberg.de**

STAGE 8
Wilhelmshöhe to Kalte Herberge

Start	Wilhelmshöhe guesthouse
Finish	Kalte Herberge guesthouse (closed Tuesdays; no food)
Distance	22.7km
Ascent	450m
Descent	405m
Time	6hr
Refreshments	Kolmenhof, Naturfreundehaus Brend (closed Mondays), Gasthaus Brend (closed Tuesdays), Gasthaus Goldener Rabe (closed Fridays), Hirschen (closed Wednesdays). Kalte Herberge is closed Tuesdays – the hotel service still operates on these days off, but there is no food available.

This stage is relaxing and easy, with minimal ups and downs but plenty of open views in all directions. The trail first runs up to a nature reserve at Blindensee and then meanders past isolated farms and hamlets to Martinskapelle. The little chapel marks an ancient sacred site near the source of the River Danube and the European watershed line between the Danube and Rhine rivers.

Westweg continues to Brend (1149m) via a tiny detour to Günterfelsen – a rocky chaos hidden in the woods. Brend doesn't seem like much of a peak, but nevertheless offers fabulous views to the south and west, especially from the observation tower. Feldberg and Seebuck can clearly be seen to the south, with the two prominent towers serving as a landmark. The last part of the day's walk, from Neueck to guesthouse Kalte Herberge runs close to the B500, which can get busy (and loud) on weekends, but otherwise does not impact the walk too much.

Pass through the Westweg portal opposite **Gasthaus Wilhelmshöhe** and follow the boardwalk across the small bog to a trail junction that has no obvious markers. Bear right and take the middle track, through the barrier and into the forest. After passing a field the trail comes to another trail junction by a crucifix (way cross), also without obvious markers. Stay on the broad track to reach *Gitschbühl* and continue along the edge of the pastures.

After passing a fire pond turn right on the paved lane (Turntalstraße). The trail passes *Blindenhöhe* and about 400m further along reaches *Blindensee*, where a small path to the left leads into the nature reserve and to the **lake**.

> **Blindensee nature reserve**, established in 1960, protects 28ha of rare raised bog habitat. The lake, which is entirely rain-fed, is almost as acidic as vinegar. Only a small number of specialised species have adapted to this hostile and nutrient-poor environment. Over the millennia the peat layer has grown to more than 7m thick – an astonishing amount, considering its growth rate of about 1mm per year! Its earliest origins thus date to about 8000BC.

Follow the boardwalk to *Brand* and turn right on the paved lane, past scattered farms and homes. At the

Blindensee

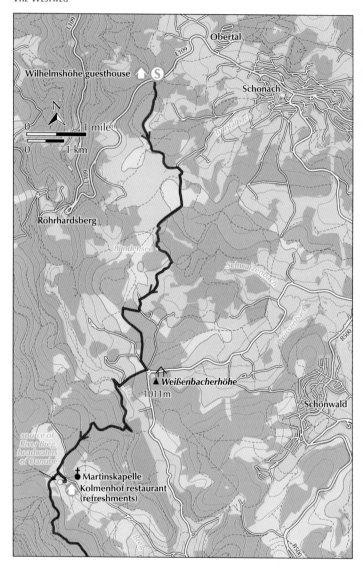

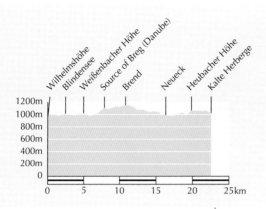

T-junction turn left and just after the bend fork to the right onto a small path into the forest. After 10m turn right to reach *Weißenbacher Wald*. Here the trail turns left along the edge of the forest. At *Farnberg* join the paved lane to the left, towards the car park and picnic area at **Weißenbacher Höhe**.

Before reaching the little hut, Westweg takes a sharp right down towards a little hamlet in the valley, and up on the other side. At *Vogte* turn left and head up towards the nature reserve *NSG Briglirain*. Here the trail turns right on Brücklerain, now a little more steeply. Shortly after passing the source of the River Elz, keep to the left at the fork to reach *Forsthaus Martinskapelle* and continue straight on to *Martinskapelle*.

The **Danube** receives its most distant headwaters from the River Breg, which has its source just below Restaurant-Hotel Kolmenhof, opposite Martin's chapel. In Donaueschingen, the Breg merges with the River Briga and together they form the Danube and start the 3000km journey to the Black Sea. Westweg does not pass by the source directly; to find it look for the sign for Donauquelle on the grounds of guesthouse Kolmenhof.

Map continues on page 117

Martinskapelle, near the source of the Danube

At *Martinskapelle* bear left and almost immediately turn right towards Brend. Just after *Kolmenkreuz*, Westweg leaves the broad track and takes a minor detour via a small trail to the right, to visit Gunterfelsen – an unexpected jumble of boulders and rocks, hidden in the forest. The path around the rocks and back to the broad track is not particularly well defined, but the general direction is quite clear. Once back on the forest road continue to the right, past *Naturfreundehaus Brend*, to reach **Brend**.

The **serenity** of this spot is not immediately obvious. You have to walk past the car park, observation tower and restaurant to reach the benches in the field on the edge of the hilltop; from this vantage point the ambience and vistas are quite enchanting. From the observation tower, which is open to the public, the views can stretch all the way to the Alps.

At *Brend* (1149m) the trail forks to the left and runs parallel to the paved lane through the trees. After passing a pasture the trail returns to the lane and follows it to a T-junction at *Alte Eck*. Turn left towards Restaurant-Gasthaus Goldener Rabe (Guesthouse Raben) and turn right at *Beim Raben*, just before reaching the **guesthouse**.

Map continues on page 119

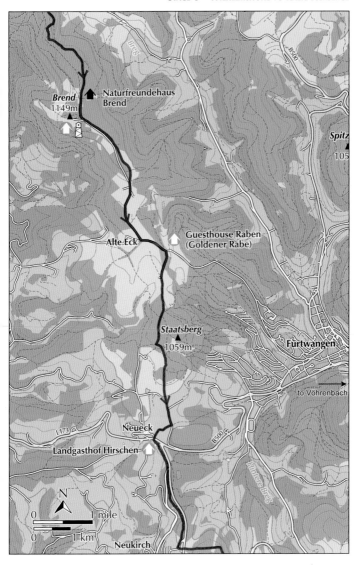

Typical farmhouse in the Hochschwarzwald

The trail runs over the soft contoured back of these mountains, passing isolated farms dotted among the rolling hills and patches of forest.

Walk straight past *Nördlicher Staatsberg* to *Winkel*, where Westweg is joined by Querweg Schwarzwald Kaiserstuhl-Rhein and turns left to *Südlicher Staatsberg*. Here the trail leaves the broad track and bears to the right past more fields and open views towards Feldberg. At *Beim Staatsberghof* turn right and head towards the big road.

At *Neueck* cross the road via the underpass and turn left past guesthouse **Landgasthof Hirschen**. The trail runs parallel to and just below the level of the road (B500). Cross a small street to the left and continue on the footpath next to the B500. Soon the trail enters a patch of trees, but still essentially runs parallel to the road. Keep to the left to reach *Am Stollenwald*.

Bear left and then right to cross the bridge over the B500. Follow the left fork into the forest and at the next fork keep to the right. The trail cuts across along the northern slope of the hill, while the B500 loops around the southern flank. On the other side pass below the big bridge and turn right towards the hamlet of **Schweizersgrund**. Follow

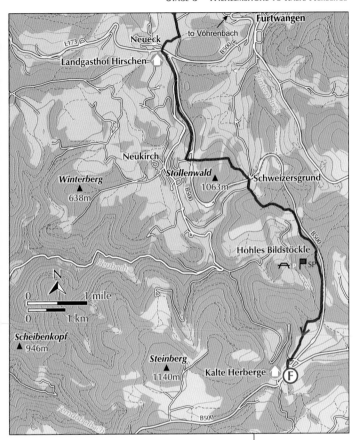

the trail to the left, up the hill and around the bend to enter the forest on quite a steep path.

At a big trail junction and timber landing, turn to the left and continue uphill on the middle track. Soon the path emerges from the forest and runs around the edge of the field to the left. At *Heubacher Höhe*, Westweg and Mittelweg meet again and jointly they head towards the road.

Continue parallel to the road, past a lay-by and picnic table at **Hohles Bildstöckle** (a signpost as well as a
Bildstöckle, which is a sort of devotional waycross). Just
after *Hochwald B500*, turn right and almost immediately
fork left onto a small path that runs around the top of the
field and back down on the other side to **Kalte Herberge**,
right by the B500 (restaurant closed Tuesdays).

VÖHRENBACH

The village of Vöhrenbach, a couple of kilometres northeast from Kalte Herberge,
epitomises the back of beyond. Who would have thought that it produced not
just one but two 'famous sons' during the era when musical automatons, the
19th-century precursors of the gramophone, were all the vogue? These two indi-
viduals (not related!) were extremely successful and one of them even set up a
workshop in London. Highly sought-after, Vöhrenbach automatons were ordered
by the Jockey Club of New York, the Sultan of Istanbul, the king of Italy and the
Royal Opera House in Covent Garden – and one was even on display at the first
world fair, 'the Great Exhibition' in London, in 1851. Today there are scant traces
of this history found at the town museum (opens on request), but some elaborate
examples of their works are displayed at museums around the world, including
the V&A in London.

Tourist information

Tourist-Information Vöhrenbach: 78147 Vöhrenbach, tel +49 (0)7727 501115,
info@voehrenbach.de, **www.voehrenbach.de**

STAGE 9
Kalte Herberge to Titisee

Start	Kalte Herberge (guesthouse)
Finish	Kurhaus, Titisee
Distance	20.3km
Ascent	330m
Descent	500m
Time	5hr 30min
Refreshments	Berggasthaus Lachenhäusle (closed Wednesday and Thursday), Gasthaus Schweizerhof (closed Mondays) Gasthaus zum Kreuz (closed Thursday), Wanderheim Berghäusle (closed Thursdays except if Thursday is a public holiday, in which case they close on Wednesday instead)

This section starts off running close to the B500, but after crossing it at Süßes Häusle the trail takes on a whole different perspective as it runs along the edge of the forest or traverses open fields, where the eyes can feast on panoramic views towards Feldberg and the Alps beyond. The day ends in Titisee (or Hinterzarten), where the route splits.

From **Kalte Herberge**, cross the B500 and walk up the hill for about 250m to *Bei der Kalten Herberge*, where Westweg heads up into the forest. After about 200m, turn left onto the field track. Walk along the edge of the field to the right, past the house and head back into the forest. Keep walking straight on to a big trail junction at *Fernhöhe* and turn right towards a lay-by. Look for a small trail that starts along the edge, in the middle of that lay-by, and runs back into the forest.

At first the path leads away from the road, but it soon returns and runs parallel to it. It crosses the trailhead car park at **Lachenhäusle** and heads back into the woods. After about 300m the trail bends to the left. ▶ Keep walking straight on, across the junction, and at the fork keep to the right. Where the track bends to the right, Westweg

There are not many markers here.

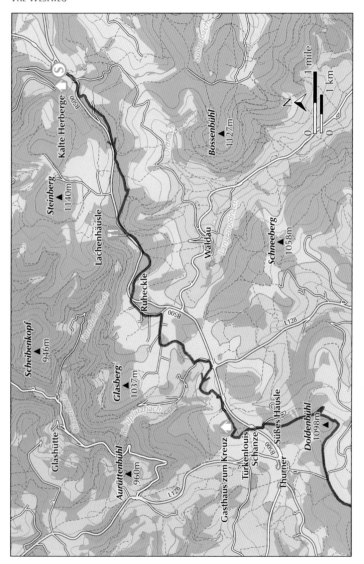

forks off to continue straight on and crosses the road. (Be careful – dangerous bend.)

Map continues on page 125

On the other side, walk along the paved lane, past *Ruheckle* and turn right at the street sign 'Glashöfe 1,2,3,6'. At *Glashöfe* turn left through the fields and back into the woods. At the trail crossing take the right-hand trail, and 10m further on follow the left fork out of the forest. Cross the field to the right. By the houses turn left to reach an underpass by the B500.

Instead of passing through the underpass, turn right and continue along the lane with beautiful panoramic views across the rolling hills and scattered farms. After the bend the trail turns sharply to the left, up a gravelly field track. By the house turn left and head towards the road, but do not cross. Bear right towards **Gasthaus zum Kreuz** and cross the car park to find the small path that leads up along the edge of the field and straight on into the woods to a trail junction by an interpretive sign about **Türkenluis Schanze** (trenches).

Open views all around on this section of the trail

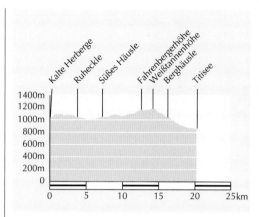

The north-south orientation of the Black Forest Mountains always seemed like a **natural line of defence**. It was fortified all along the central ridge stretching for more than 160km north to south. However, it rarely succeeded in its intended purpose of fending off advancing French troops. The hardship of war and defence – as always – was borne by the local people, who had to serve in corvée labour and endured pillaging, raids and battles. The last battle took place here in 1796, when the Austrian army tried to fight back French troops that had advanced into Swabia.

Turn right on the grassy trail to *Hohlen Graben*, then walk along the edge of the field to the left. Cross the road and walk down the lane towards the forest.

At *Süßes Häusle*, Westweg turns left and heads off into the forest, still on the paved lane. A few metres further along, by another sign called *Süßes Häusle*, fork to the right, onto a forest track. The trail soon reaches a large open field at *Doldenbühl-Schanze* and runs around the edge of the field to the right. This is a very scenic trail with open views across the southern Black Forest.

After passing a hut the trail eventually goes back into the forest and reaches a fork, where it leaves Allmend Fahrenbergweg. Continue straight past *Wildmoos* to a triangle junction. Cross the first track and at the second crossing track continue to the right. The trail leads out of the forest and across the fields on a gravel track to **Fahrenberger Höhe** (1132m). At the top of the hill, an odd-looking designer bench makes a great viewpoint. ▸

Feldberg and its neighbours fill the horizon.

Turn left across the fields, and at the top return to the forest. Follow the bend down to a forestry road and turn left. (There are no signs here.) After about 350m, just before a bend, Westweg takes an unexpected left turn

Map continues on page 126

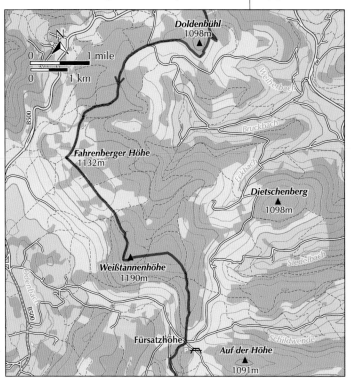

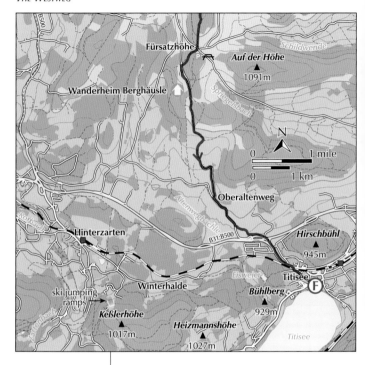

and starts to climb up to *Weißtannenhöhe* on a small, steep path. Cross the forest road and continue straight on to a junction at *Holzwaldweg*. Follow the forest road to the right and out of the forest to the trailhead car park at **Fürsatzhöhe**.

Look for a trail that starts on the right-hand side of the car park and runs straight through the forest to **Wanderheim Berghäusle**. After passing the Wanderheim and some other buildings, the trail continues to the right and leads down into the valley through the fields. Hinterzarten, with its huge ski-jumping ramps, lies to the right and Feldberg dominates the backdrop.

At *Oberaltenweg* turn left and continue down into the valley. Just before the big road (B31), turn left

along a little stream and pass the golf course. Cross the stream and pass underneath the bridge to reach **Titisee**. Head down the street and cross the train tracks via the subway to Alte Poststraße; continue straight down to *Strandbadstraße* and turn left to reach *Kurhaus*.

The tourist hotspot of Titisee comes as a bit of a shock after all the solitude

TITISEE

Titisee is one of the most popular tourist spots in the Black Forest. Situated picturesquely on the region's largest natural lake, and framed by some of its highest peaks, the kitsch-factor is undeniable – but so is the beauty of this setting.

During the summer Titisee is very busy and a favourite bathing spot. To make water fun available year-round, a huge indoor pool with 'wannabe' tropical island ambience has opened its doors – complete with palm trees, water slides, and a wellness section. Something for everyone!

Tourist information

Tourist-Info Titisee: Strandbadstr. 4 79822 Titisee-Neustadt, tel +49 (0)7652 12068100, titisee@hochschwarzwald.de, www.titisee-neustadt.de

Tourist-Info Hinterzarten: Freiburger Straße 1, 79856 Hinterzarten, tel +49 (0)7652 1206-8200/8204, hinterzarten@hochschwarzwald.de, **www.hoch-schwarzwald.de**

Badeparadies Schwarzwald: Am Badeparadies 1, 79822 Titisee-Neustadt, tel +49 8000 4444333, **www.badeparadies-schwarzwald.de/en**

EAST OR WEST?

At the end of Stage 9 Westweg splits into an eastern and a western approach to Basel (see 'Walking the Westweg' in the main introduction). Traditionally, the eastern route circles around Lake Titisee and heads to Bärental – a forgettable place by a busy road junction – while the western route heads over to Hinterzarten, just over the hill to the west.

If you want to take the eastern route, but also want to visit Feldberg – the highest mountain of the Black Forest – you have a couple of options:

1   If you're determined to climb Zweiseenblick, the mountain above Bärental from where it is possible to get a distant glimpse of both Titisee and Schluchsee at the same time, you can stay in Titisee or Bärental and continue to Feldberg via the traditional eastern route (Zweiseenblick), and insert another day to explore Feldberg before continuing south to Weißenbachsattel (see Stage 10B).

2   You could give Zweiseenblick a miss and instead continue to Hinterzarten and Feldberg with the western route and reconnect with the eastern route at Feldbergpass (Hebelhof/Grafenmatt Parkplatz) (see Stage 10A).

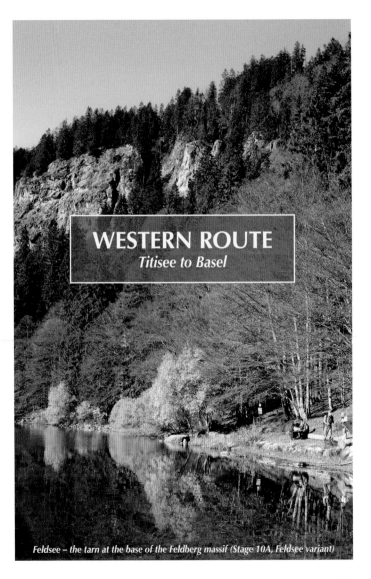

WESTERN ROUTE
Titisee to Basel

Feldsee – the tarn at the base of the Feldberg massif (Stage 10A, Feldsee variant)

STAGE 10A
Titisee to Notschrei

Start	Kurhaus, Titisee
Finish	Notschrei
Distance	25.6km
Ascent	850m
Descent	580m
Time	7hr 30min
Refreshments	St Wilhelmer Hütte (closed Wednesdays), Gasthaus Stübenwasen (closed Thursdays); via Feldsee: Raimartihof (open Nov–June except Tuesdays), restaurants at Seebuck

The trail crosses a smallish hill between Titisee and Hinterzarten and arrives at one of the most dramatic spots in the vicinity, right next to the huge ski-jumping ramp that is Hinterzarten's landmark. A small path leads steeply down to Oberzarten from where the trail ambles easily up the valley, past mountain pastures and deep spruce forest to Rufenholzhütte. Here the trail splits into two: the right-hand trail (main route) leads up steeply to Grüblesattel, right between Seebuck and Feldberg. From Grüblesattel the trail heads over to the weather station to continue via St Wilhelmer Hütte and Stübenwasen (1386m) to the mountain pass at Notschrei. On clear days, when the Alps are visible, the panorama is amazing; only the last bit, from Gasthaus Stübenwasen to Notschrei, runs through the forest. The left-hand trail will take you to Raimartihof (Guesthaus) and Feldsee – the tarn at the base of Feldberg – before climbing up to the commercial area at Seebuck and Feldbergerhof where it rejoins the main route. Both variants are described here (there is little difference between the two in terms of distance and ascent), along with an option to link up with the eastern Westweg route at Stage 11B.

The trail to Hinterzarten continues right opposite the *Kurhaus* at **Titisee**. Take the small footpath down to 'Bootshaus Café direkt am See' and walk along the lake and through the Kurpark to the outdoor swimming pool, where the trail returns to the road at *Titisee/Strandbad*.

Turn left to *Tannfried* and follow the small trail to the right, around the back of some houses up the hill and into the forest.

Soon the path emerges at the back end of a little housing precinct. Continue to the corner and turn left for about 100m and look for a little footpath just below the campground that runs behind a building into the fields. Pass the fire pond and circle around the campsite to the right, and at the top end of the property turn right along the fence to *Oberhalb Campingplatz Bühlhof*.

Turn left, through the forest. At *Bühlberg* fork to the left. The trail comes to a field and runs along the edge of the forest to *Bankenhansenkreuz*. Turn right, back into the forest towards Keßlerhöhe (marked by a sign on a tree); soon the trail reaches the **ski-jumping ramp** above Hinterzarten.

Cross the access road to *Scheibenfelsen*, where there is a viewpoint with a couple of well-placed benches. Take the small, steep path to the left, down through the forest. At the bottom turn left on the paved lane and at

Hinterzarten: the unlikely centre of summer ski-jumping

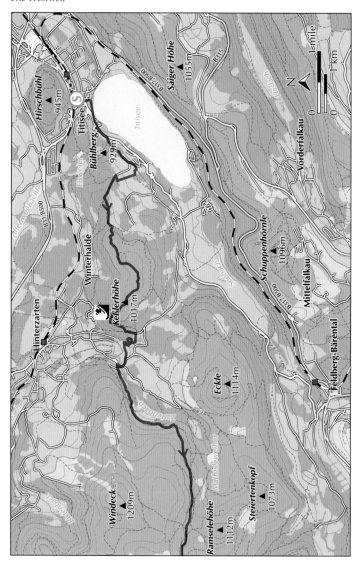

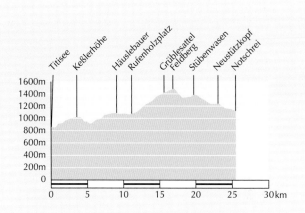

Hellblech follow the small path (Keßlerhangpfad) in front of the villa down to *Keßlerhalde*.

The main village of Hinterzarten lies to the right. Westweg crosses the pasture at the top end of the valley over to Oberzarten. Pass the big farm (Keßlerhof) and follow the bend of the road around to *Keßlerberg*.

Walk up towards Hotel Sonnenberg and continue on the field track that runs gently up the valley. Pass the fire pond and keep going straight on into the forest. After passing *Stuckwald*, briefly join the forestry road to the right (80m), then fork to the left. This track immediately splits and Westweg branches to the right, slightly uphill, to another forest road. Turn left for about 100m. Here the trail again branches off to the right onto a smaller trail. At the fork keep to the left. Continue straight on until the trail joins a forestry road to the left and reaches a big open valley at the base of Feldberg.

After passing the farm at *Häuslebauer*, turn left at *Fürsatzmoos*. Pass *Landratshütte* and keep to the left. Just after the little bridge at *Rufensteg* the trail splits: follow the right-hand track on Rufenhofweg to reach a shelter hut by a big trail junction at **Rufenholzplatz**. Here Westweg splits into two variants, with the main

Map continues on page 134

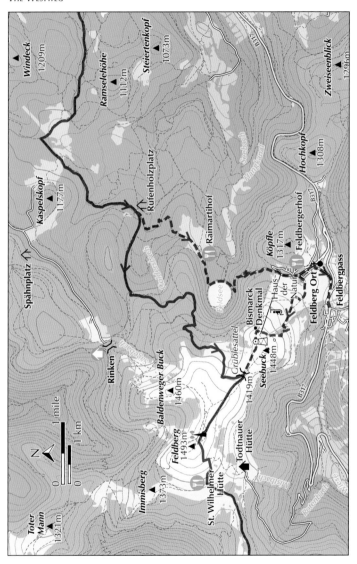

(right-hand) route heading to Grüblsattel, and the alternative (left-hand) route taking in Raimartihof guest house, Feldsee and Seebuck (see 'Variant via Feldsee', below).

For the main route, pass to the right of the hut on Rufenlochweg. After about 400m the trail forks to the right and starts climbing uphill, to a forestry road at *Seewald*. Briefly turn left and look for a small path on the right. Follow that trail up the back of the tarn wall above Feldsee. ▶

This trail may be muddy and slippery at times; proceed with caution.

Eventually the trail levels out and runs through quite open terrain to a junction. Bear right to reach *Unterm Grüble* and continue up the hill to the right (left fork). Before long the trail leaves the forest and emerges just below the saddle, with sweeping views all around. Continue to **Grüblesattel** (1419m), between Seebuck and Feldberg.

The top of **Feldberg** is an open expanse, crisscrossed by access roads and trails, and not particularly pretty, as mountaintops go. To the left is Bismarck-Monument and Feldbergturm – originally a broadcasting tower of the SWR (TV/radio station) that is now used as an observation tower. For a small fee you can climb an additional 45m to the viewing platform for even more sweeping views.

To link with the eastern route to Basel (2.2km, 22m ascent, 159m descent)

Those wanting to continue on the eastern route can turn left at *Grüblesattel* and head towards *Bismarckdenkmal* and down to '**Haus der Natur**' via a small path that starts near the cable car mountain station. By *Haus der Natur* turn right, past the parking garage and branch off to the right past **Feldberg chapel** to reach Feldbergpass, by the **B317**. The eastern route continues on the other side of the road at *Hebelhof/Grafenmatt Parkplatz* (see Stage 11B).

Variant via Feldsee

At **Rufenholzplatz** take the left fork to *Am Goldersbach* and then follow the small path through the woods to the

Map continues on page 138

135

Feldsee, at the foot of the Feldberg

right. After about 800m the path reaches a trail junction above **Raimartihof**. Continue straight down the track past Raimartihof to *Oskar-Andris Eck*. Leave the broad track and continue straight on to **Feldsee**. By the lake turn left and start climbing up the hill; at the top turn left to reach the base of Seebuck.

SEEBUCK

The base of Seebuck is the commercial centre of Feldberg (also often referred to as Feldberger Hof, after the Hotel of the same name, opposite Haus der Natur), with restaurants and sports shops, ski lifts and even a cable car. At the other end, by the car park, the strange hangar-like structure is 'Haus der Natur', the nature interpretation centre and tourist information.

Tourist-Information: Feldberg-Ort, Dr. Pilet-Spur 4, 79868 Feldberg, tel +49 (0)7652 12060, feldberg@hochschwarzwald.de, www.hochschwarzwald.de/Feldberg#/page/1

To join with the main eastern route, continue straight past the restaurants to *Haus der Natur*, where the trail meets the other variant that comes down from Feldberg. Just after the parking garage turn right, past the **chapel** down to Feldbergpass. Cross the road to *Hebelhof/Grafenmatt Parkplatz*.

To rejoin the main western route take the trail that starts next to **Haus der Natur** up the hill to *Bismarckdenkmal* and *Grüblesattel*.

To continue on the main route to Notschrei, turn right at **Grüblesattel** and climb up towards the weather station at *Feldberg* (1493m). The path does not go up to the actual summit, which is just a little bit further up, by the observation platform.

St Wilhelmer Hütte – a popular spot with great panoramic views

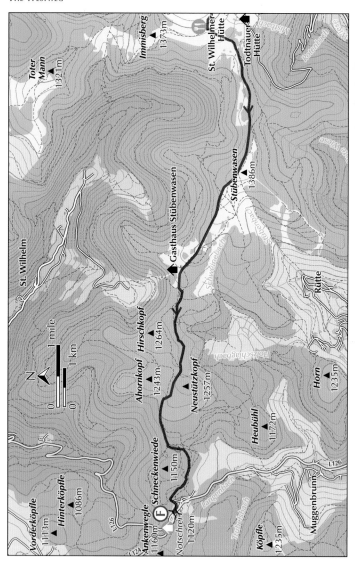

Head down the hill between the TV mast and the weather station, past *Oberhalb Todtnauer Hütte* to reach **St Wilhelmer Hütte**. ▶

Cross the yard and follow the access road to *St Wilhelmerhüttenweg*. Bear right on the forest track towards **Stübenwasen** (1369m) – a long-drawn ridge with fabulous open views to the south.

This is a very **popular trail** for both walkers and mountain-bikers, especially on weekends. At Stübenwasen there's a huge 'tree bench' – a gigantic tree trunk laid down flat with nest-like 'sun beds' carved into it that serves as a viewing platform.

Walk across the ridge, past the tree-bench, to **Gasthaus Stübenwasen**. Cross the lane and walk straight on along the edge of a pasture. At the far corner bear left and follow the forest road to the right, to *Langmoos*. Keep walking straight on, down the hill. Soon after passing *Neustütz* the trail turns left onto a paved lane that leads to the Sparkassen Arena – a Nordic sports training facility. Pass the Arena and turn right at *Spänplatz* to follow the paved lane down to **Notschrei**.

The terrace at St Wilhelmer Hütte has the best views of the southern Black Forest, the Vosges and the Alps on the distant horizon.

NOTSCHREI

Notschrei is just a mountain pass with not much going on during the summer. But it really springs to life in winter, when skiers and Nordic combiners come from all over to play in the snow. There is only one, fairly expensive wellness hotel, right by the road. Gasthaus Stübenwasen has some simple rooms and more options for accommodation can be found at Muggenbrunn, Todtnauberg, or Hofsgrund, below Schauinsland, a couple of kilometres up the road.

Tourist-Information Notschrei: Passhöhe Notschrei/Loipenhaus, 79674 Todtnau, tel +49 (0)7652 12060, notschrei@hochschwarzwald.de, www.hochschwarzwald.de/Todtnau

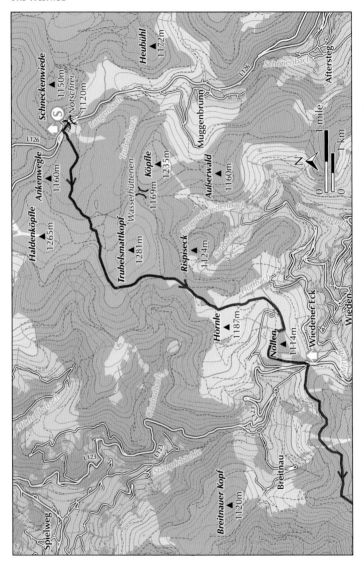

STAGE 11A

Notschrei to Haldenhof

Start	Notschrei
Finish	Haldenhof (guesthouse)
Distance	18.9km
Ascent	605m
Descent	790m
Time	5hr 30min
Refreshments	Wiedener Eck (closed Mondays and Tuesdays), Belchenhaus
Note	Many of the small trails around the top of Belchen are closed during the winter.

This is a rather gorgeous section of the Westweg. The trail climbs through the forest around Trubelsmattkopf and then crosses open mountain pastures on its way down to the pass at Wiedener Eck. From here it climbs to Heidstein and down again to Krinne, where the steep ascent up to Belchen's summit starts. Belchen (1414m) is often considered the most beautiful mountain in the Black Forest, thanks to its gorgeous 360° views. On the way down the trail passes the Hohkelch saddle and runs through gnarly mountain beech forest to Gasthaus Haldenhof (Neuenweg).

At **Notschrei**, cross the road and head towards the cross-country ski hut (Loipenhaus) at *Beim Notschrei* and follow the gravel track towards Wiedener Eck. The trail passes through a nature reserve that protects a raised bog.

> This **peat bog** was commercially used until 1947 (visible to the left). Today it is kept open and is regularly cleared of brush to provide a habitat for rare bog species.

After about 1km, at a left bend, Westweg leaves the gravel track and continues straight on, into the forest on

Map continues on page 143

141

Langenbachweg. Pass *Trubelsmattkopf*, now on a narrower trail which leads to a forestry road and crosses to the left. Continue to *Münsterweg* and turn left. After passing *Glashofwald* the trail reaches a shelter hut at *Auf den Böden* and bears to the right. Walk along the edge of a pasture and soon the trail crosses open fields with great views of Belchen and Hörnle. Eventually it heads towards a couple of big farms, but before reaching them bear left and head down the hill towards the road.

At **Wiedener Eck** cross the road and head for the Westweg portal. Follow the dirt road just next to it gently up the hill. After passing under a ski lift watch out for a marker pointing to a small trail on the left. Climb uphill through the forest, cross the forest road and continue on a small path up the hill on the other side to another forest road. Turn right for about 150m and then branch off onto a smaller trail again (marked by a nature reserve sign) and continue up the hill to *Am Heidstein*.

After crossing what looks like an old tree chute the trail eventually emerges from the forest by a timber

The trail above Wiesental

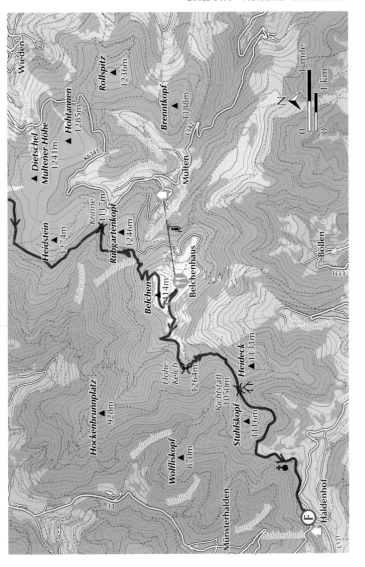

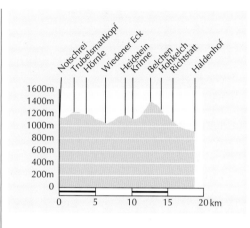

landing, where the view opens up towards Belchen and Hohkelch straight ahead, and Hochblauen a bit further away in the distance. Turn left. The track gradually morphs into a small path as it runs down to **Krinne** – a major trail junction near the road (car park, picnic hut).

Turn right and take the small serpentine trail on the left for the final ascent to the top of Belchen. ◄ After climbing for about 2km the trail comes out of the forest and you are greeted with sweeping views across the entire southern Black Forest and the Alps beyond. Feldberg is over to the left.

Here the trail splits. Westweg continues straight on, around the base of **Belchen** to the hill station of the cable car at Belchenhaus. To get up to the summit climb a little bit further up the hill on the yellow marked trail. The bottom part of this trail is very eroded, but it soon joins a gravel path to the summit.

To get down to Belchenhaus you can follow that gravel track in either direction as it connects with Belchenrundweg – a circular path around the base of the summit. If you cross the peak to the west, Westweg branches off the Rundweg just before reaching **Belchenhaus**; if you come down on the eastern slope

This trail is closed during the winter, and on the north face of Belchen snow and ice can persist for quite a long time – sometimes well into May.

the trail comes out by the cable car station and passes **Belchenhaus**.

Look for a gravel trail (Belchenrundweg) next to the wooden information board. After a few metres Westweg branches off to the left to cross the slope and heads over to the **Hohkelch** saddle. (This trail is closed during the winter.)

At *Hohkelchsattel*, turn towards the forest, to the right. Pass through the gate on the left and head down the hill on a rugged trail through elfin beech forest. (This trail is also closed during the winter.) Soon the path reaches a forestry road and joins it to the right, passing *Alte Grenzmauer* on the way to the trail junction and shelter hut at **Richtstatt**.

Cross the junction to the right and continue on the broad forest road past *Metzg* and *Spänplatz*, with beautiful views across Wiesental along the way. After passing **Dekan Strohmeyer Kapelle** (chapel) the trail reaches a car park at *Im Mond*. Cross the small hillock to the right, past a couple of houses, to reach **Haldenhof**.

Belchenhaus, café and mountain station of the Belchen cable car

145

HALDENHOF (NEUENWEG)

Haldenhof is a convenient stop-off point on the way to Kandern and the only guesthouse in the vicinity. If you still have energy, you might like to visit Nonnenmattweiher – a little tarn lake just 3km from Haldenhof.

Tourist-Information Belchen: Neustadtstraße 1, 79677 Schönau im Schwarzwald, tel +49 (0)7673 918130, info@schwarzwaldregion-belchen.de, **www.schwarzwaldregion-belchen.de**

Overnight alternative: Badenweiler

If all the rooms are fully booked at Haldenhof a good alternative would be to take the bus down to Badenweiler (May–Oct, three buses per day), a historic spa town that dates back to Roman times. The ruins of the Roman bath temple have been preserved as a museum, and are located in the Kurpark, right next to the modern spa. The park, which was established some 200 years ago during Badenweiler's glory days, is a botanical gem featuring many interesting exotic species. Towering above the park, and spectacularly overlooking the Rhine Valley, sits Burg Badenweiler – a medieval castle ruin that was destroyed during the Franco-Dutch War (1672–1678).

Tourist-Information Badenweiler: Schlossplatz 2, 79410 Badenweiler, tel +49 (0)7632 799300, touristik@badenweiler.de, **www.badenweiler.de**

Cassiopeia Therme: Ernst-Eisenlohr-Str. 1, 79410 Badenweiler, tel +49 (0)7632 799200, therme@badenweiler.de, **www.badenweiler.de/Cassiopeia-Therme**

STAGE 12A

Haldenhof to Kandern

Start	Haldenhof (guesthouse)
Finish	Tourist information office, Kandern
Distance	19.8km
Ascent	470m
Descent	1050m
Time	5hr
Refreshments	Blauenhaus, Restaurant Maien in the village of Vogelbach (off-route; closed Tuesdays)

This stage runs mostly through the forest, but there are gaps here and there, especially in spring or autumn, when leaf cover is not full. After climbing up to the mountain pass at Kreuzweg the trail runs relatively level most of the way to the Egerten hut, where the final ascent to Hochblauen (1165m) begins. Hochblauen (often simply called Blauen) is the last significant mountain along this route and provides one last opportunity to take in the beautiful mountain panorama before descending down to Kandern and the rolling hills of Markgräflerland. Shortly before reaching Kandern the trail passes Sausenburg – a romantic castle ruin with far-ranging views across the region.

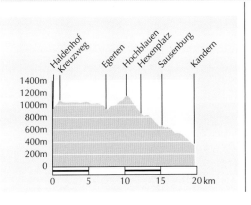

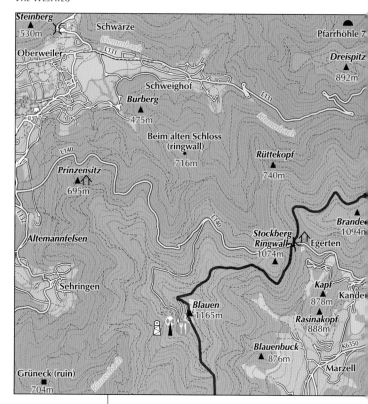

Map continues
on page 152

Walk up the street past the car park opposite **Haldenhof**.
At the bend, Westweg branches off and crosses the field.
At the top it cuts off the hairpin bend of the road and con-
tinues on a small path that leads into the forest towards
Weiherkopf.

    After about 170m an old sign announces 'Kreuzweg
1.9km', but don't let this confuse you. Westweg takes a
shorter route by taking the trail to the left, which leads out
of the forest and across a field/ski slope, above the road.
Head for the ski lift to reach a bus stop and large trailhead
car park at Kreuzweg.

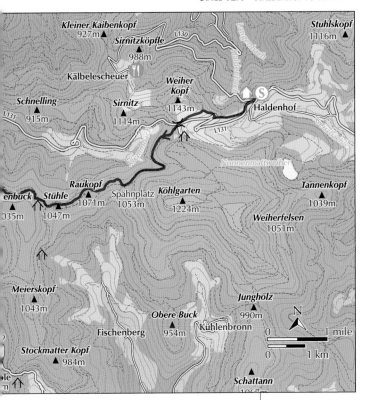

Cross the road to the right to *Kreuzweg* and look for the small trail by the road that runs off into the woods towards 'Waldwirtschaft Wanderheim Stockmatt' and *Spähnplatz*. The trail soon merges with a forest road that leads down to a big trail junction. Take the right-hand fork (Höhenweg) around the tight bend and continue on the broad forest road to a hut by another big trail junction at **Spähnplatz**.

Cross the junction and walk down the rough track opposite for about 5m, then turn right onto a small trail (Meyerskopfspur). ▸ This briefly touches a bigger track,

Between 1 November and 15 July please stay on the trail to protect endangered wildlife.

but almost immediately turns off to the right again on a small path. However, this is not immediately obvious, as only the yellow marker is clearly visible, along with a sign pointing towards Stockmatt.

The trail reaches **Stühlehütte hut** by a big forestry road junction at **Stühle**. Cross to the right and follow the big forestry road (Stühle Egertenweg) for a few metres, then branch off to the left again onto a small path. There are not many markers; the trail just continues straight on, almost level, occasionally crossing other tracks until it gently descends to the **Egerten hut**, by a small road.

Cross the road and look for the small path by signpost *Egerten* that immediately begins to climb up the hill. After about 350m join the track to the left, which in turn joins another, bigger track to the left. About 75m further along, Westweg forks to the right and continues up the hill.

The memorial commemorates a couple of French military pilots, who crashed their plane here in May 1964.

Cross the trail junction at *Stockberg* and keep heading uphill to *Fischerbrunnsattel*. Continue straight on to the fork and take the right-hand trail up the hill, which soon reaches the access road at *Vorder Hochblauen*, just below the radio transmitter. Turn left along the road for about 30m, to a memorial stone. ◄

Continue on the steep little trail up, past the paraglider take-off point and a well-placed picnic table, to reach the observation tower Aussichtsturm Hochblauen (**Blauen**) (1165m).

The **observation tower** was built by the Schwarzwaldverein in 1895. There's a pay booth, which is staffed during the summer. Admission fee for adults is €0.50. The sweeping panoramic views from the top are quite impressive, with Belchen and other peaks rising in the north and east, the undulating hills of Markgräflerland rippling towards Basel and the craggy line of Alpine giants along the southern horizon.

In front of the building is another nice, open and sunny, south-facing spot, perfect for gazing at the Alps, which also serves as a take-off site for paragliders.

Cross the hilltop to **Hochblauenhaus**, on the southern periphery, by the car park. ◄ Look for the small

trail that starts by Blauenhaus and ambles back into the woods, heading south, down the hill.

Cross a forest road (Neuer Blauenweg) and continue straight on to a trail junction at *Hägi*. Cross half-right and continue on the trail opposite. At a tight bend there's an old wooden sign that reads 'Jetzt gang I ans Brünnele', which indicates a spring, but Westweg continues around the bend and down the hill (there are no markers here). Just before reaching the bottom the trail unexpectedly turns left and takes a small path towards a little shelter hut (Hexenplatzhütte), by the trail junction at **Hexenplatz**. ▶

Cross Hexenplatz junction to the right and continue on the broad forestry road (Käsacker) to *Unter Hexenplatz*, where Westweg branches to the left onto another fairly big track (Hexenplatzweg) leading down to *Gümppen*. Continue down the hill to the right on a forest track and soon after fork to the right. After passing *In den Riesen* the trail emerges from the forest by a lay-by at *Lindenbückle* by the village of **Vogelbach**.

View from the top of Hochblauen, back towards Belchen

On 16 March 1978 a small aircraft crashed here; on board it had the mayor of Montbeliard in France.

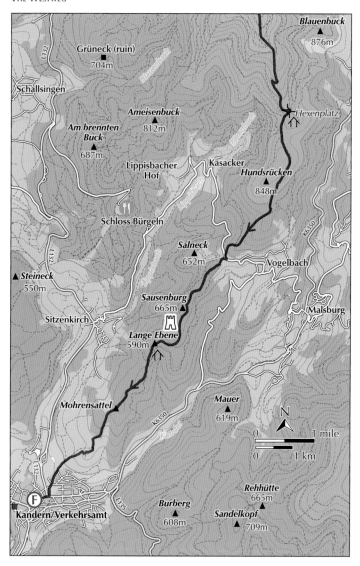

Cross the road, pass the houses and walk down the field track. After about 30m branch to the right, and continue through the forest. At the fork keep to the left, down the hill. By a picnic table take the trail to the left up to the **Sausenburg ruin**.

View of Markgräflerland from Lindenbückle

Burg Sausenburg dates back to AD1232, but it was never a particularly important stronghold compared to the much more imposing Burg Rötteln. Sausenburg suffered greatly during the Thirty Years' War: it was first occupied by imperial forces, and then by the Swedes, but in 1678 the French laid waste to it, as they had done to Burg Badenweiler and Burg Rötteln. Climbing up the tower is well worth it for the sweeping views of Markgräflerland. Close the doors when leaving and do not enter this (or any other) tower during a thunderstorm.

Sausenburg ruin, above Kandern

Return to the trail and continue down the hill to **Lange-Ebene-Hütte shelter hut** and straight on, past Kanzelweg to *Lange Ebene* trail junction. Take the right-hand fork to follow Mohrensattelweg to *Wässerliwald*. Follow the left fork to a pasture at **Mohrensattel** and continue straight on, quite steeply down the hill.

Mohrensattel marks the **fault line** along which the tectonic plate cracked, thus simultaneously creating the Rhine-graben and causing the mountains to lift. The bedrock of the mountain massif is visible to the left, while the rift valley spreads to the right. It appears relatively shallow due to the sediments and debris that have filled it up through the eons.

The trail emerges from the forest and lands you softly among the fruit orchards of Markgräflerland. Where Mohrensattelweg becomes paved and bends to the right, Westweg continues straight on and follows a track just inside the woods. Just before reaching a pasture the trail forks to the right and ambles down to an access road.

Keep to the left as you walk down the hill. Pass *Im Loh* and head towards the church. Take the one-way street (Oxengasse), past the church, down to the main street of Kandern. By Gasthaus Ochsen turn right to reach the tourist information office (*Verkehrsamt*) at *Kandern/Stadtmitte* in the centre of **Kandern**.

KANDERN

Set amid vineyards, orchards and hills, Kandern epitomises quintessential Markgräflerland. The busy little market town is famous for its pottery tradition, which is founded on the proximity of the local clay pit. An annual pottery market takes place in September. The expressionist painter August Macke (1887–1914) captured Kandern's timeless idyll in many of his works. A themed trail leads to some of his most famous motifs.

From 1895 to 1985 a railway line connected Kandern and Basel. During the summer the historic steam engine still runs part of the route on Sundays (www.kandertalbahn.de). Timetables and reservations are available at the tourist office.

Tourist-Information Kandern: Hauptstraße 18, 79400 Kandern, tel +49 (0)7626 972356, verkehrsamt@kandern.de, **www.kandern.de**

STAGE 13A
Kandern to Basel

Start	Tourist information office, Kandern
Finish	Basel Badischer Bahnhof, Basel
Distance	26.4km
Ascent	480m
Descent	565m
Time	6hr 30min
Refreshments	Alte Krone (Wollbach) (closed Tuesdays), Burgschänke (Rötteln castle, closed Sundays and Mondays)
Note	Be sure to have your passport with you, as this stage takes you over the border into Switzerland.

Westweg's final stage is not lacking in highlights. Just beyond Kandern lies the first surprise of the day: Wolfsschlucht – a small but impressive gorge that began its existence during the Jurassic age as a coral reef, submerged in warm, shallow waters. The trail continues through the undulating vineyards, orchards and wine villages of Markgräflerland, before returning to the forest for the last time. Its emergence high above Lörrach, on the doorstep of Burg Rötteln, is as surprising as it is dramatic. Framed by green hills all around, Basel wells up from the valley below. But instead of heading straight for the urban jungle Westweg skirts around the edges of civilisation and reaches its final destination via Tullinger Berg, by the most scenic approach possible.

At *Kandern/Stadtmitte* in **Kandern**, head towards the back of the tourist office (*Verkehrsamt*), cross the square to the right and cross the bridge over the River Kander. Turn right along the river to Hammersteiner Straße and cross this big road (L134) by bus stop 'Staigasse'. Walk down the little street opposite (Papierweg, also bike trail Kandern-Hammerstein). Immediately after crossing the Kander again, turn right, cross the railroad tracks and head up the hill.

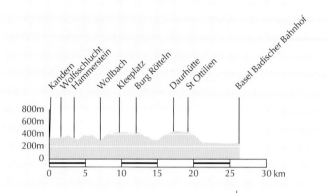

At the fork keep to the left. At *Hebelbrünnli* turn right and climb up to a T-junction at *Wolfsschlucht*. Turn left and immediately left again to enter the **gorge**.

The path leads through the gorge, composed of mysterious limestone cliffs and rock formations. In the centre

Wolfsschlucht, remnants of a Jurassic coral reef

157

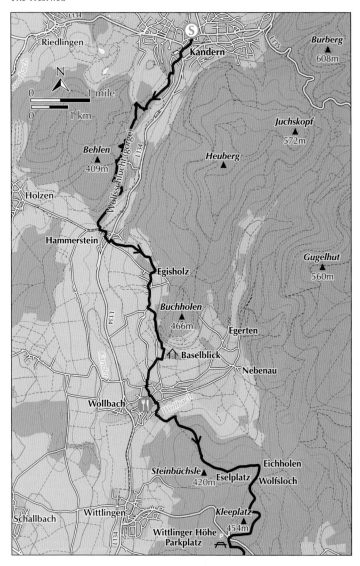

it opens up to a large clearing and picnic area. After a narrow passage the trail leaves the gorge and continues through the forest to a trail crossing. Turn left to another junction where old signs point the way to Kandern, Holzen and Hammerstein. Follow the path towards Hammerstein down the slope to the left.

At *Brudersloch* turn right onto the broad forest track. After about 200m, at *Burgholz*, take the small trail to the left. Before reaching the country lane at the end, the trail forks left across a little bridge and comes out by a farm. Walk towards the street (*Hammerstein/Unter der Burg*) and turn left to cross the railway tracks. By the water fountain at *Hammerstein/Am Dorfbrunnen* turn right to *Hammerstein/Im Döfli*, and then head up the hill on Kammlenweg.

Cross the big road (L134) and turn left onto a little access road (Rebstallweg). After 20m turn right and follow the field track up towards the edge of the forest. At the fork turn right to *Egisholz*. Bear right and by the village (**Egisholz**) turn left, past the houses straight across the crossroads. About 250m after leaving Egisholz turn left and follow the edge of the forest to reach a **shelter hut** at *Baselblick*.

Turn right, down through an orchard to another track. Here turn left, and immediately right again onto a grassy path across another orchard to a T-junction at *Himmelsliege*. Turn right, cross the access lane and walk straight down the hill past the cemetery and *Wollbach/ Ob dem Rathaus*.

Pass to the right of the *Rathaus* (town hall) and walk down Rathausstraße, around the church and down to *Wollbach/Kronenplatz*, by Gasthaus Alte Krone. Cross Nebenauer Straße and continue on Röttler Weg up the hill towards the forest. The paved lane ends by the edge of the forest and Westweg turns left on Steinbüchsleweg. After about 150m turn right, uphill, and go straight on to a T-junction at **Eselplatz**.

Turn left to *Eichholen*, where Westweg joins the Schwarzwald bicycle route to the right, towards Wittlinger Höhe. At *Wolfsloch* turn right for about 50m to

Map continues on page 161

159

Map continues
on page 162

another signpost also called *Wolfsloch* and fork to the left on Kleeplatzsträsschen – a smaller track that avoids the bicycle traffic but leads to the same trailhead car park.

At **Wittlinger Höhe** (car park) cross the road and follow the track (Hohe Straße) to the right of the car park into the forest. At *Trimm-Dich-Pfad* pass through the barrier on the left and follow the fitness trail to *Am Trimm-Dich-Pfad*, and 20m further on branch to the left onto a smaller path. At the end pass through the barrier at Schloßhalde and join the broader track to the left to arrive at the back of **Burg Rötteln**.

> The exact origins and age of the **castle** are not known, but it is believed to date to about the 11th century. Along with Sausenburg and Burg Badenweiler it formed the seat of power of the Margraves of Baden in Markgräflerland. All three castles were destroyed on the same night, on 29 June 1678, during the Franco-Dutch war. A small entrance fee is charged to gain access to the museum and upper castle (www.burgruine-roetteln.de).

Burg Rötteln

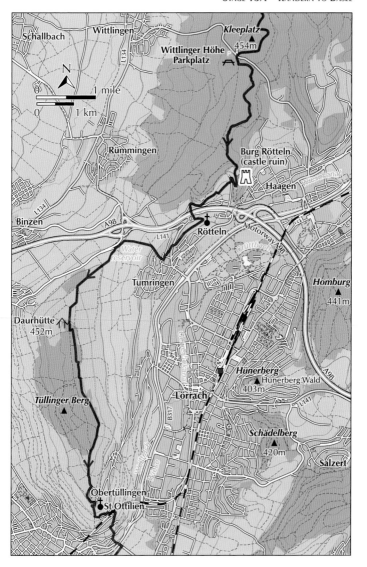

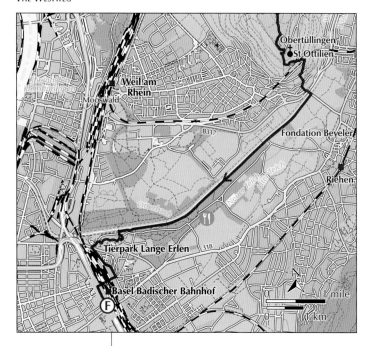

Follow the trail on the right, through the gate and past restaurant Burgschänke down to the car park. Here you'll find the final Westweg portal. Turn left, and just after the car park look for a track that runs through the orchards and gardens to the right.

After passing below the power lines the trail comes to a T-junction and briefly turns right, then bears left and passes under the power lines again before reaching *Oberhalb Kirche Rötteln*. Turn left and pass through the subway under the motorway to **Kirche Rötteln**. Pass the church and follow the bend to the left.

The lane leads to the outskirts of **Tumringen**. At the edge of the residential area bear right and continue on Oscar-Grether-Straße. At the end cross Freiburgerstraße to the left and fork to the right on Burgstraße. Join Wittlinger

Weg to the left, to *Tumringen/Engel*. Follow Luckestraße up the hill to the right and out of the village.

Pass the orchards to reach a **water reservoir** tank. Turn left to a picnic spot at *Beim Wasserreservoir Tumringen*. Here Westweg forks to the left and heads up to *Luisenhof*. Fork left again, and after about 100m follow the fruit tree-lined broader path to reach the picnic hut at **Daurhütte** on the edge of Tüllinger Berg.

Daurhütte is a nice place to take a break, offering **sweeping views** across Markgräflerland, the Rhine Valley and the Vosges on the other side, as well as Burg Rötteln and Hotzenwald to the northeast.

Continue straight on, past the hut to signpost *Daurhütte*. Turn left to the next bend and then follow the edge of the hill to the right, all the way to the other end, at *Tüllingen/Lindenplatz* – a popular picnic spot overlooking Weil am Rhein, Basel and Lörrach.

Bear right across the car park and follow the little lane past the meadow. At the T-junction turn left through a housing complex. By the big sign pointing towards 'Ottilienkirche, Obertüllingen, Grenzübergang Riehen/ Schweiz', turn right.

Ottilienkirche, the little church perched on the side of the hill above Riehen belongs to a **trinity of chapels** dedicated to three virgins, who are said to have been followers of St Ursula. Although little is known about the historic origins of these chapels, the sites on which they stand are thought to have been sacred sites since pre-Christian times. The other two chapels in this triplet are St Chrischona on Dinkelberg – an important early Celtic site – and St Margarethen near Binningen in the south of Basel.

Narrow steps lead down the hill to *Am Tüllinger Berg*. Turn left, cross the road and walk alongside it for about 20m, then turn right, into the vineyards. Bear right at the fork and at the T-junction. Pass through the barrier – you have just crossed into Switzerland!

Follow the trail to the left on a zigzag route down the hill through the gardens and vineyards. (Watch out for sudden left turns down some narrow steps that may easily be missed.) The path passes a little water fountain and bench then continues down the hill on some more steps. (Use both the red Westweg markers as well as the Swiss yellow markers, often painted on trees, for orientation.)

Finally the trail reaches the road by a natural pool/leisure centre (Naturbad Riehen). Turn left across the bridge and change to the other side of the street. The last part of the trail runs next to the river almost all the way to Basel Badischer Bahnhof station (about 1hr 15min or 5km). Ignore all bridges or turn-offs.

This final approach is surprisingly pleasant and green. After passing a café (Schliessi) by a lock, the trail reaches a little bridge (Erlenpark Steg), where Westweg finally turns off to the left and meets Erlenparkweg at a

Basel Badischer Bahnhof – the end of the trail

T-junction. There is no Westweg marker here, so follow the Swiss hiking trail signs to the left. Shortly afterwards you'll be surprised to find yourself at the gates of a little zoo – **Tierpark Lange Erlen**. The Swiss trail marker points straight at the gates, which can be confusing if you reach this point after hours and find the gates locked.

The trail does in fact run through this little zoo, bearing right after the gates. At the other end it comes out on Erlenparkweg again. Turn left towards the big road and cross Fasanenstrasse. Bear left, and immediately turn right on Im Surinam along the railway tracks to reach a big junction. Turn right and pass under the railway bridges to reach the station (**Basel Badischer Bahnhof**) and the end of Westweg. ▶

This station is run by Deutsche Bahn. The bigger, international station is Basel SBB on the other side of the Rhine.

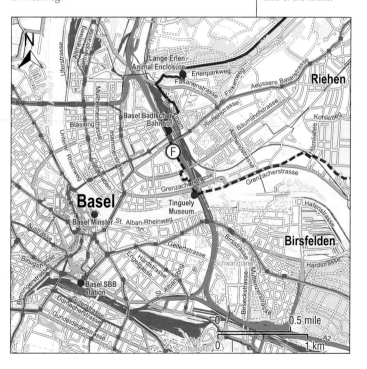

BASEL

Basel is a bustling city with many facets. To round off your walk a short stay here is highly recommended. There are many interesting sites in and around the city, many of which can be explored on foot. The city tourist board has published a brochure that guides visitors along some self-guided and clearly waymarked 'city walking routes' to the most interesting sites (ask at the tourist office).

Basel Tourismus is located in the Stadtcasino, at Barfüsserplatz, and in the SBB train station. Tel +41 (0)61 268 6868, info@basel.com, **www.basel.com/en**

EASTERN ROUTE
Titisee to Basel

The Menzenschwand Valley (Stage 10B)

STAGE 10B

Titisee to Feldbergpass

Start	Kurhaus, Titisee
Finish	Hebelhof/Parkplatz Grafenmatt (tourist information), Feldbergpass
Distance	14.4km
Ascent	541m
Descent	164m
Time	4hr 30min
Refreshments	Schwarzwaldklause, Hotel Adler (Bärental)
Note	The classic route has Stage 10 run all the way to Weißenbachsattel, but this is a very long way and does not allow for any exploration of the Feldberg massif. The route described here breaks the section into two stages, with this one ending at Feldbergpass.

The eastern route splits off by the Kurhaus in Titisee and runs along the shore of the lake, passing some campgrounds on the way to the train station of Bärental. Here the trail starts climbing up to Zweiseenblick (1296m), from where Lakes Schluchsee and Titisee can be glimpsed in the distance, before ambling down the southern side of the hill to Caritas House. For the last couple of kilometres the path runs parallel to, but below the level of the B317 to Feldberg.

This stage is not very long. To make the most of the day, climb up to Haus der Natur (nature interpretation centre) at the base of Seebuck and follow 'Feldbergsteig' to Feldberg summit and down to Wilhelmer Hütte, to enjoy the views. Strong walkers may want to complete the well-marked circuit via Zastler Hütte, Baldenweger Hütte, Raimartihof and Feldsee, and back up to the commercial centre at Feldberger Hof. The full route is 12km long and takes at least 4hr.

From *Titisee/Kurhaus*, head towards the centre of **Titisee** and turn right on the pedestrianised lake-front promenade, past the boat landings to Hotel *Seehof*. Cross the

hotel car park and follow the footpath along the shore to the southern end of the lake, where a campground seemingly obstructs the way. Ignore the barrier and walk right

Lake Titisee

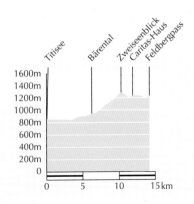

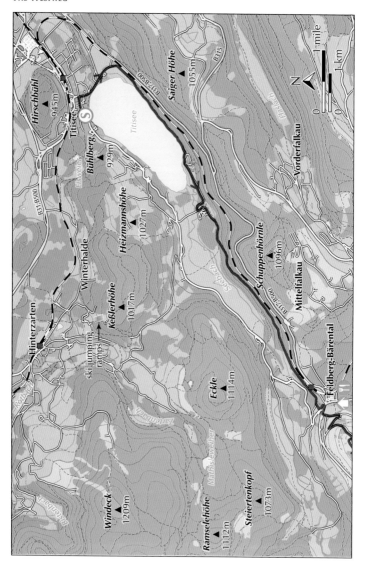

through the campsite, past the reception hut and out at the other end.

Follow the paved lane to another campground (*Campingplatz Bankenhof*) and pass it to the left. Shortly after, pass yet another campsite, Jugendzeltplatz Bankenhof. Keep to the left and continue on a regular forest trail, mostly uphill to **Bärental station**.

Walk past the station (*Bärental Bahnhof*) and by the wooden information board fork to the right on Tannenweg. After about 100m, at *Bärental/Tannenweg*, turn left and left again just before the road. Pass the pond and cross the B317 via the subway. On the other side bear right and walk up the steps to Schrofenweg.

Continue straight on to a little chapel (*Benezkapelle*) and follow the lane around to the right on Im Dobel. At the T-junction turn left on Zweiseenblickweg and head up the hill. After passing the Clubhouse of SC Feldberg fork to the right and cross the fields. The trail re-enters the forest and reaches a big trail junction at *Happ*. Continue straight on for about 20m, then branch to the right. At

Old signpost in Titisee; follow the clock carrier

Map continues on page 172

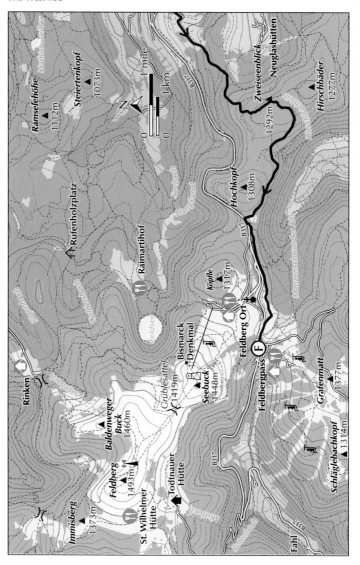

Hirschbäder briefly turn right, and after 20m bear left for the final ascent to **Zweiseenblick** (1292m). The viewpoint (*Aussichtspunkt*) is just to the left. ▶

After taking in the views return to the signpost and continue straight across the trail on which you arrived, and follow the small footpath through a patch moor. On the other side follow the regular forest track down past a shelter hut (*Hochkopfhütte*) and straight on to *Caritas Haus*, right by the road, above the Menzenschwand valley. Bear left and look for a trail that leads downhill past the playground. By the football pitch fork off to the right and continue parallel to the road to Menzenschwander Hütte at **Feldbergpass**. *Hebelhof/Parkplatz Grafenmatt* (information) is in the car park to the right.

From this vantage point it is possible to get a glimpse of both Titisee and Schluchsee, hence the name Zweiseenblick, which translates as 'two-lake view'.

FELDBERG

Feldberg, which became popular long before people cared about sustainable tourism, is a victim of its own popularity. What can be seen here is the ugly face of unfettered development. Feldberg is busy year-round, but during the winter visitor numbers explode, as this is the most popular ski area in the Black Forest.

Tourist-Information (Haus der Natur): Feldberg-Ort, Dr. Pilet-Spur 4, 79868 Feldberg, tel +49 (0)7652 12060, feldberg@hochschwarzwald.de, **www.hochschwarzwald.de/Feldberg#/page/1**

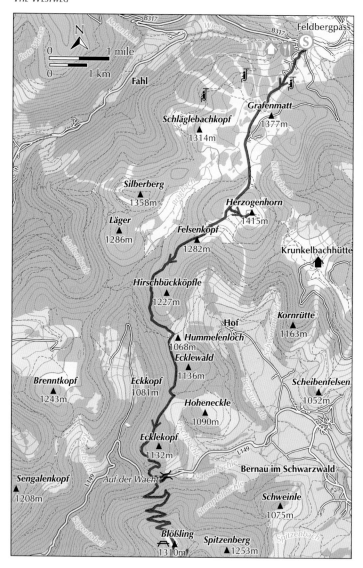

STAGE 11B
Feldbergpass to Weißenbachsattel

Start	Hebelhof/Parkplatz Grafenmatt, Feldbergpass
Finish	Gasthaus Auerhahn, Weißenbachsattel
Distance	18.5km
Ascent	720m
Descent	875m
Time	5hr
Refreshments	Gasthaus Emmendinger Hütte, Berggasthaus Grafenmatt (closed Thursdays), Gasthaus Herzogenhorn (all at the start of the route)

This is where the two branches of Westweg separate for good. The eastern trail heads south and climbs Herzogenhorn (1415m), which is far less busy than Feldberg yet offers similarly wonderful 360° views. The trail continues down to Wacht at 973m before climbing steeply up to Blößling (1310m). But the effort is worthwhile as quiet rewards await at the top: good picnic spots with beautiful views. The rest of the way to Weißenbachsattel follows the ridge most of the way, but skirts around most of the peaks – except for Leder-Tschobenstein (1212m). Shortly before Weißenbachsattel the trail passes Hochkopf (1263m), which can be climbed via a short, steep detour.

At *Hebelhof/Parkplatz Grafenmatt* by **Feldbergpass**, Westweg starts heading south towards Herzogenhorn. Bear right at the fork and head up the hill on the gravel trail. Cross the paved driveway by Gasthaus Emmendinger Hütte and continue on the small footpath next to the bench, up the hill past Berggasthaus Grafenmatt, the ski slopes, Gasthaus Herzogenhorn and 'Bundesleistungszentrum' – an Olympic training facility.

At *Glockenführe* continue straight on towards **Herzogenhorn**. However, the trail does not climb to the top; to make the worthwhile detour turn left at *Schwedenschanze*. ▶

Map continues on page 177

Thanks to its bald top, Herzogenhorn offers great panoramic vistas.

Herzogenhorn

At *Schwedenschanze* Westweg continues on the grassy field track straight down through the pasture. (By the interpretive sign a little footpath goes off to the right, to a well-preserved sconce dating to 1672.) After passing a little cabin on the right the trail comes to a T-junction at *Bernauer Skihütte*. Follow the gravel track to the left

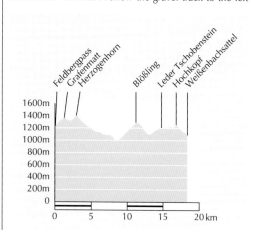

through the forest (Schwarzbrunnenweg) to a shelter hut at Hofeck.

Turn right towards the signpost *Hofeck* and continue on the gravel track (Ecklewaldweg) towards Blößling. At the T-junction turn right on Roterfelsenweg to reach Roter Felsen – a viewpoint with a conveniently placed bench facing Blößling. Continue down the hill and cross the road at *Wacht*.

On the other side Westweg starts trudging up on Blößlingweg – a rather tedious gravel track that leads up

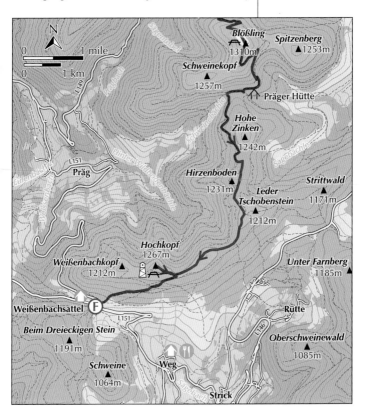

the hill on steep serpentines. By a bench close to the top, Westweg branches off sharply to the right and follows a small footpath to the peak of **Blößling** (1310m).

Cross the top of the hill, past the picnic hut and descend on another serpentine trail down to *Blößlingsattel*. Turn sharply to the right to follow a narrow footpath down the side of the hill. Almost at the bottom, join the gravel track to the right to reach a **shelter hut** (Prägereckhütte) at Präger Eck. Turn right and head down the grassy track through the nature reserve to Schweinekopfweg.

Turn left onto the forestry road and keep to the left at the fork, heading up the hill. Where the path levels out Westweg leaves the broad track and continues climbing towards Leder Tschobenstein, now on a small path. Shortly after this, Westweg branches to the right. Ignore the red arrows on the trees and keep walking straight on. (There are few markers here.) The trail opens up and becomes a kind of ridge trail, and through the trees you catch small glimpses of the surrounding scenery. Eventually the path reaches **Leder Tschobenstein** (1212m), at a trail junction.

If you're wondering what the **leather jacket and stone** hanging up there in the tree are supposed to mean, you're not alone. It appears to be an attempt to express the name of this mountain literally. The name, which probably ranks as the oddest place name in the whole of the Black Forest, is: *Leder* (leather), *Tschoben* (Alemannic word for jacket) and *Stein* (stone). However, this does not really explain anything and nobody seems to know how the mountain got its odd name.

Still following the ridge trail, continue straight on towards Hochkopf – the last peak of the day. Westweg

Hochkopfturm observation tower, just above Weißenbachsattel

179

bypasses the actual summit, but it's only a short detour to get to the top: just follow the yellow marked trail at *Am Hochkopf* – a steep and rough track which clambers uphill for about 500m to reach the **peak** (1267m).

Back at *Am Hochkopf* bear left on the broad track and after about 100m Westweg suddenly forks off to the left and takes a more direct (and steep) route down through the trees, crossing another forest road along the way. At the bottom the trail reaches a small gravel lane at **Weißenbachsattel**. Head towards Gasthaus Auerhahn (Hochkopfhaus), on the right at the bend.

WEISSENBACHSATTEL

Weißenbachsattel is in the middle of nowhere, 2km away from the nearest village. Gasthaus Auerhahn is the most convenient option for accommodation, but other alternatives can be found in the idyllic little village of Todtmoos-Weg, just a couple of kilometres down the road. (Follow Westweg markers to the high ropes course, then continue along the road to the village.)

STAGE 12B
Weißenbachsattel to Hasel

Start	Gasthaus Auerhahn, Weißenbachsattel
Finish	Hasel/Oberdorf signpost, Hasel
Distance	22km
Ascent	345m
Descent	980m
Time	5hr 30min
Refreshments	None on route

This section runs almost entirely through the forest, much of the time on forestry roads, offering few views. However, just before starting the climb up to Hohe Möhr (984m) the trail briefly emerges from the forest, giving way to lovely views of Dinkelberg, Basel-Land (2L), and on clear days some Alpine peaks. Hohe Möhr itself is entirely covered by trees; to get the wonderful views you will have to climb the observation tower. This is the last real peak of the eastern route; from here the trail descends into 'civilisation', first passing through the little village of Schweigmatt and ending the day in Hasel.

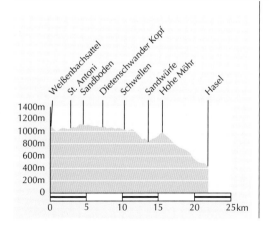

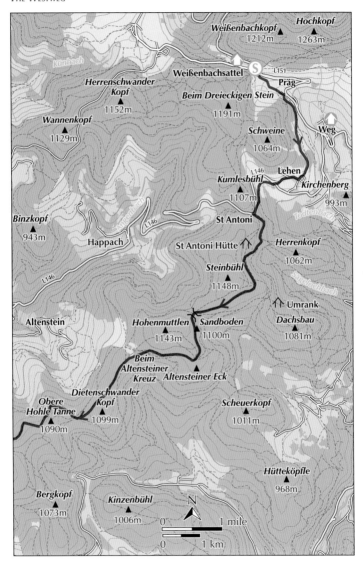

St Antonihütte

From **Weißenbachsattel** follow the road around the bend towards Todtmoos. The Westweg portal is right by the road, but the trail actually branches off across the field just before it. Walk along the ski lift down the hill to the base station, pass the high ropes course and turn left to follow the field track that runs parallel to the road. The trail reaches the outskirts of **Lehen** and bears right to pass the houses.

Walk to the street corner and turn right on Alpenblickstraße. By the crucifix fork to the left, taking a small path to cut off a little bit of the road. Cross the country road to the left and continue on Im Kaltwasser, past the house and through the field to a Y-junction at *Kaltwasser*. Take the right fork up to the trailhead car park at **St Antonipass**.

Cross the car park and follow the forest road to the left to the **shelter hut** at *St Antonihütte*, by a large trail junction. Pass the hut to the right to *Umrank*. Take the right-hand fork, slightly uphill on Hohmuttelweg. (There are not too many markers here.) Keep going straight for about 2km to reach a barrier by a large forest road junction at **Sandboden**.

Map continues on page 185

Old boundary stone marking the borderline between Markgräflerland and Fürstenberg territories

Cross the junction to the left and follow the gravel track to a timber landing at *Altensteiner Eck*. Walk straight across and continue on Mittlere Straße. By some cross-country ski trail signs (*Loipen*) follow the right-hand fork on the grassy track to Altensteinerkreuz Weg to reach *Altensteiner Kreuz*.

Turn left and take the small track through the forest. Belchen comes into view to the right, through the trees. At *Belchenblick*, Westweg branches to the right to reach a large forest road junction at *Sägbaumdumpf*. Cross the junction and continue on the broad forest road to the right, on Mittl. Rohrbergweg. Shortly afterwards, fork to the left on Oberer Rohrbergweg, which leads to the crossroads at **Schwellen**, where the trail emerges from the forest.

Follow the paved lane to the right. On the other side of the field, at Hörnli, the trail continues on a field track along the edge of the forest, with beautiful open

Map continues on page 186

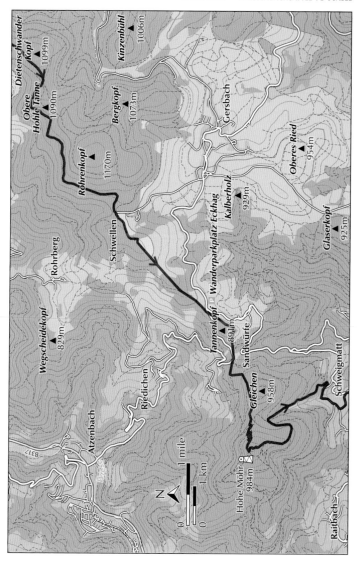

views to the south. Pass the model airfield and continue straight on, down to a car park and picnic spot at *Wanderparkplatz Eckhag*.

Cross the road to the car park and follow the track up the hill. At the fork keep to the left. Watch out for the unexpected marker pointing to the left, towards a field. Continue along the edge of the field. Soon the trail rejoins the track and just before a bend, forks onto a small trail to the left, heading steeply down the hill to *Tannenkopf*. Follow the gravel road to the right and join the paved road to left, around the bend to Sandwürfe.

Continue along the road for a few metres more and take the following track to the left, uphill to

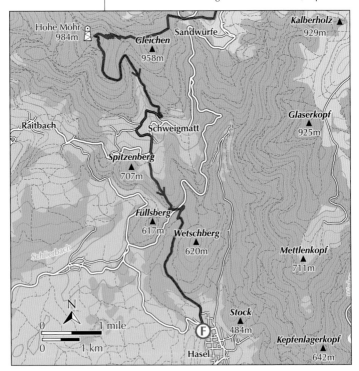

Schwatternwald. Turn left to reach *Am Gleichen* and join the gravel track to the right, which terminates at a timber landing. Keep walking straight, on a slightly overgrown track, where right away Westweg branches off to the left and heads up the hill on a small path that leads to a hut (Rotruhhütte) at a bend at *Rotruhe*.

Turn left up the hill on the gravel track for about 150m and watch out for a small zigzag path on the left that starts climbing up the hill on steep serpentines. By the TV mast at the top, turn left to the picnic area and observation tower at **Hohe Möhr** (984m).

To admire the **views** you will have to climb the observation tower. On a clear day the views towards the Alps, across Wiesental, Dinkelberg and Markgräflerland are beautiful, even from this modest height.

From here the trail runs downhill all the way to Hasel. Westweg leaves Hohe Möhr on a small trail behind the tower, which joins a forest road to the left to reach a hut at *Kastendycktanne*. Follow the bend around and out of the forest along the edge of a valley.

At *Beim Waldhaus* the track turns into a paved lane and passes at the back of the guesthouse to the main village of **Schweigmatt**, passing *Schweigmatt/Schwimmbad* and *Bühlmatt* on the way. At Schweigmatt follow the bend around to the left to reach a bigger country road. Cross the road and walk down the hill for about 200m.

Just before the car park turn left past the horse ranch and follow the lane around an S-bend to the end of the village, where the paved lane turns into a field track. At the fork continue to the left. Just inside the forest the trail becomes a thin path that skirts the edge of the hill. It briefly crosses a wider track, but immediately continues through the undergrowth on the other side to reach a forest road at *Füllsberg*.

Right behind the signpost the trail continues on a small, steep path down through the forest. Cross the road to the left and continue on the other side (not a good

Ambling down into Markgräflerland

place for wearing shorts) above a stream. The trail reaches a gravel track and follows it around the bend to the left. Continue straight on. (There are no markers.) Ignore any trails going off to the left or right, and at the trail crossing take the right-hand fork down the hill, past the water tower to reach *Hasel/Oberdorf* in **Hasel**.

HASEL

The little backwater community of Hasel is home to a geological curiosity: Erdmannshöhle – one of Germany's oldest limestone caves. The cave is some 2185m in length, but only 360m of it are accessible to the public. It can be visited during the tourist season, from April to November.

Erdmannshöhle: Wehrer Straße 25, 79686 Hasel, tel +49 (0)7762 80689-0

Tourismus Info Hasel: Bürgermeisteramt, Hofstraße 2, 79686 Hasel, tel +49 (0)7762 80689-0, info@gemeinde-hasel.de, **www.gemeinde-hasel.de**

Südwärts Tourist Information: Hauptstrasse 23, 79650 Schopfheim, tel +49 (0)7622 396145, tourismus@schopfheim.de, **www.suedwaerts.com**

STAGE 13B
Hasel to Degerfelden

Start	Hasel/Oberdorf
Finish	Wolfsgraben, Degerfelden
Distance	24.4km
Ascent	410m
Descent	545m
Time	6hr
Refreshments	Berghaus Hohe Flum (closed Thursdays and Fridays)
Note	There is no accommodation in Degerfelden, but a regular bus service runs to nearby Rheinfelden, where there are many options.

This section runs pleasantly through undulating fields and orchards. Soon after leaving Hasel the trail passes another geological curiosity, which may or may not be visible: a mysterious lake that appears and disappears depending on the groundwater level. The highest point of the day is Hohe Flum – a nice picnic spot with an observation tower. After passing Oberminseln the route takes a turn for the worse, due to the construction of a new motorway (A98). Westweg is currently rerouted to run right next to the motorway for about 600m to Nöllinger Tunnel, where it heads off into the woods again. In the middle of the forest it passes the remains of an ancient Roman villa before taking a rather secret approach through Wolfsgraben ravine to the outskirts of Degerfelden.

At *Hasel/Oberdorf* in **Hasel**, follow Hauptstraße to the right, to the end of the village, where the trail branches off to the left on an old field track that runs parallel to the road, around a bend and up into the fields. After crossing a track it meets the road again. Join it to the left for about 20m, then turn left again, heading straight towards a horse ranch.

Walk through the farmyard and head back into the fields. At the field track crossing, turn right to reach a

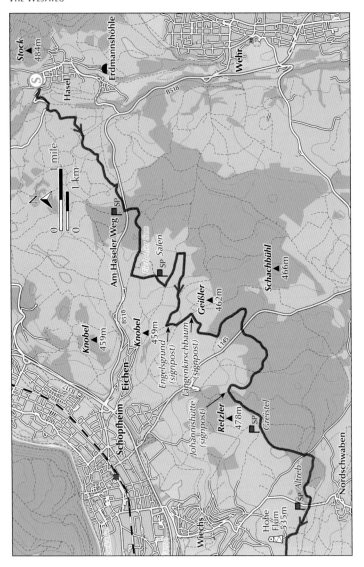

paved access lane. Cross the lane to the left and continue on the other side through the field. After the bench the track bends to the left, heading south and slightly uphill. After passing a small stand of trees, turn right into another field. Continue to the left, along the edge of the field.

The track ends by another paved lane; turn right and at the bend continue straight on, on the field track, running parallel but at some distance to a road. After passing a small patch of trees the track comes to another paved access lane and turns left. Before reaching the road turn off to the right again and continue parallel to the road.

Undulating folds of Dinkelberg

Map continues on page 193

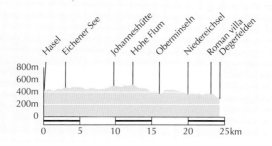

Hohe Flum – a good place for a picnic

At *Am Haseler Weg* climb the small steps on the left and carefully cross the road (bend!), and continue straight into the forest on Seehölzleweg. By a trail junction at *Im Seehölzle* branch to the right. Soon the trail emerges from the forest by **Eichener See**.

> The **lake** may or may not be visible. Most of the time it resides underground, but when groundwater levels rise the lake can grow up to 2.5m deep! Despite its erratic nature it is home to a rare prehistoric crustacean known as the fairy shrimp (*Tanymastix lacunae*).

Pass the 'lake' and turn left at *Am Eichener See*. From here the trail takes a zigzag route through the fields and orchards. At the T-junction at *Salen* turn left, and at the following trail junction turn right. Follow the bend to the right then merge with the access road to the right, to a T-junction at *Engelsgrund* on the edge of Eichen. Turn left and left again on Langen Kirschbaumweg at the next T-junction. At the next trail junction turn right, circling around a fruit orchard, then follow the bend to the left and head into the woods.

At the trail T-junction turn left and follow the track through the forest. After bending to the right by a timber landing the trail crosses a small road and continues on the track opposite. Cross Metzgers Egertenweg and continue on the path opposite out of the forest. Follow the bends of the field track to another trail junction at *Johannishütte*. Turn left onto the forest road to *Greistel* and continue on Greistelweg along the edge of the forest to a T-junction.

Briefly join the paved lane to the left, then, by a bench (Westwegbänkli) fork to the right and head up through the woods on a small path. Bear right. The trail reaches an orchard and continues down the hill, past a picnic hut and trailhead car park to reach a country lane at *Altreb*, just above Nordschwaben.

Cross the street and follow Höhenwanderweg. By a mile stone cross the paved lane and head straight up through the field towards the observation tower and picnic area at **Hohe Flum** (535m).

Map continues on page 195

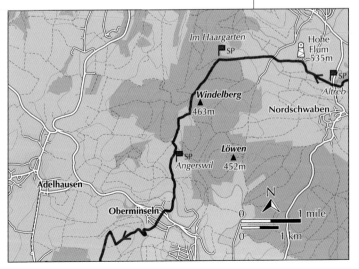

The forest is a riot of colour in the late autumn

Cross the hilltop to the left and walk down to a T-junction by a little car park. Turn right to a water fountain at *Blattenbrünnli*. Walk straight past the fountain and bear left to follow the second paved lane downhill through the fields. Enter the woods and follow Adelhauserweg to *Im Haargarten*, where Westweg forks to the left to reach a large trail junction at *Auf den Heidengräbern*.

Look for a small trail to the left that leads to a big field. Walk along the edge of the pasture to the right. By the crossing at the bottom, turn left for 100m to *Angerswil*, then follow the lane up the hill to the right. Walk straight across the top and head towards the village.

Pass straight through **Oberminseln**, past *Zum stillen Winkel*, and follow Moosmattenstraße up into the fields. At the T-junction turn right and follow the field track up and then bending to the left, across the top of the hill. Just before the overhead power-line turn right, and at the next crossing left again. The track meets a paved lane at a T-junction. Turn right and at the following T-junction right again. After about

100m Westweg branches off to the left and heads gently downhill; after a further 600m turn left on Übergenderweg to *Buhrenboden*, by the edge of the forest.

ROUTE NOTE

At the time of writing (summer 2016), Westweg is diverted due to the construction of a new motorway. The following is a description of the diversion. If in doubt, follow current signposting.

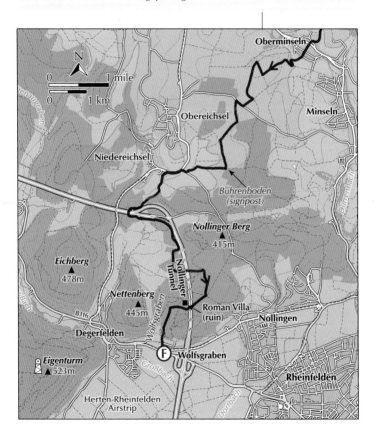

Turn right, down to a little chapel and bear right towards the road. Walk along the big road towards the village of **Niedereichsel**, to the left. Before really entering the village turn left on the very first lane, Paradiesweg, and follow it to the edge of the forest. Bear right, heading towards the A98 motorway. Pass under the motorway bridge and turn left, next to the motorway. After about 600m the motorway disappears into a tunnel and Westweg bends to the right to reach a trail crossing at *Römischer Gutshof*. Walk down Gutshofweg to the right to reach the remains of a **Roman villa** in the middle of the forest.

These **remains** are the traces of one of the most significant Roman villas that have been found on the German side of the Rhine. It is assumed that the villa was an outpost of Augusta Raurica – the ancient Roman settlement near Rheinfelden, in Switzerland.

Remains of Roman Villa

Pass the ruins and look for a small trail that branches off to the right and heads into the woods. The trail soon

joins a bigger track to the left and runs along the edge of **Wolfsgraben** ravine, down to *Wolfsgraben*, just outside Degerfelden.

> **Degerfelden** is a sleepy village between Rheinfelden and Lörrach. There are no guesthouses in Degerfelden. To get to Rheinfelden continue straight on at *Wolfsgraben* for about 100m, where you'll find a bus stop (Degerfelden/Wolfsgraben) with service to Rheinfelden or Lörrach.

RHEINFELDEN

There are two Rheinfeldens, facing each other across the Rhine. The Swiss Rheinfelden has the prettier old town and also a nice spa. It can easily be reached via a footbridge across the river and is definitely worth the excursion. Accommodation is available on either side, but is less expensive in Germany.

Nearby Augst is the site of the ancient Roman city of Augusta Raurica, which at one point had some 15,000 inhabitants. A number of ruins can be seen spread across quite an extensive area and there is also an interesting museum.

Rheinfelden Tourist Information (Germany): Karl-Fürstenberg-Straße 17, 79618 Rheinfelden (Baden), info@tourismus-rheinfelden.de, **www.rheinfelden.de/en/Tourism**

Tourismus Rheinfelden (Switzerland): Stadtbüro, Marktgasse 16, 4310 Rheinfelden, tel +41 (0)61 835 5200, tourismus@rheinfelden.ch, **www.tourismus-rheinfelden.ch/de/welcome**

Augusta Raurica: Giebenacherstr. 17, CH-4302 Augst, tel +41 (0)61 5522222, **www.augustaraurica.ch/en**

Sole Uno Spa: Parkresort Rheinfelden, Roberstenstrasse 31, CH-4310 Rheinfelden, tel +41 (0)61 8366611, info@parkresort.ch, **www.parkresort.ch/de/sole-uno**

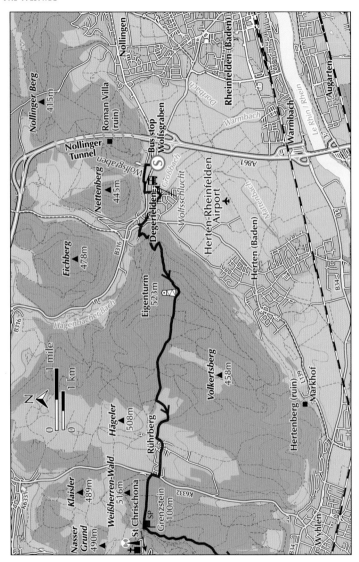

STAGE 14B

Degerfelden to Basel

Start	Wolfsgraben, Degerfelden
Finish	Basel Badischer Bahnhof, Basel
Distance	17.3km
Ascent	390m
Descent	425m
Time	5hr
Refreshments	Rührbergerhof (closed Tuesdays)
Note	If you want to skip the traffic into Basel a better option would be to finish the walk in Grenzach. At Grenzach/Bettinger Straße simply turn left and head straight down the hill on Bettinger Straße to Hauptstraße, past the town hall, across the B34 and to the station.

The final approach to Basel takes an unexpected turn. Most of the altitude metres of this stage are tackled within the first hour of the walk, with a steep climb up to Eigenturm (523m). The rest is easy, and mostly downhill, bridling the Swiss border down through the Ruschbach valley to Grenzach. This valley and the forested fringes above Grenzach-Wyhlen are botanically unique in Germany, providing a habitat for the country's only natural box wood forest. At Hornfelsen (Grenzach Horn) the trail crosses over into Switzerland and the signposting changes as the familiar red marker suddenly vanishes and yellow Swiss trail markers take over. The last 4km are quite stressful as the transition from nature to traffic mayhem comes all too suddenly.

At *Wolfsgraben*, cross the footbridge and head towards the apartment buildings. Walk through the car park and before reaching the far end cross the road and follow Nettenbachstraße to *Degerfelden/Langgärten*. Cross the bridge and turn right, along the stream. After crossing another bridge the trail runs through the old centre of the village, past some peculiar sculpture installations. The trail crosses the stream again and briefly turns

Map continues on page 202

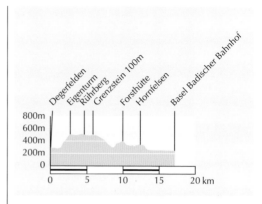

Although Eigenturm is only 523m high, it is a steep climb.

left. At the next corner turn right on Am Berg towards Eigenturm. ◀ (Follow wooden signs for Eigenturm if you can't see a red marker.)

After about 100m take the small path to the left. At the fork, Westweg forks sharply to the right and reaches the edge of the forest. The trail clambers up the hill and through the trees to a forest road. Turn left for about 100m and just before the bend look for an unexpected right turn onto a small trail that takes the most direct route up to the **observation tower** at the top of the hill.

Cross the top and head down again to *Eigenturm* signpost (512m), where the trail splits. Continue straight on, past a big trail crossing at Kreuzeichweg. At the fork, keep to the left. Turn right on Schwanderkreuzweg and pass the crucifix by the bench. At the bend, Westweg forks onto a smaller trail and continues straight on, to the edge of a field. After crossing the field re-enter the forest to reach a T-junction at *Hugenwald*. Turn right, out of the forest and through the orchards to **Rührberg village**.

At *Rührberg/Rührbergweg* walk down the hill towards the village. At *Rührberg/Rührberger Hof* turn right and follow Inzlinger Straße out of the village to a T-junction. Turn right for about 50m, then cross the road and continue through the forest on Chrischonaweg to *Grenzstein 100m*, by the Swiss border. Instead of crossing

Pumpkin harvest in Rührberg

into Switzerland, turn left down the hill on Rudishauweg to *Wyhlen/Ziegelhof*.

View across Whylen

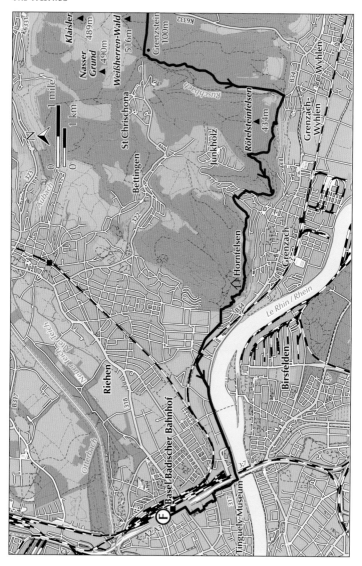

At *Rudishauweg* a small trail marked as an alternative Westweg route through Ruschbachtal branches to the right. ▶ The trail is marked with yellow markers and rejoins the regular route at *Rustel*.

At *Wyhlen/Ziegelhof* turn right by the street lamp and follow Ziegelhofstraße up the hill and back into woods. At *Am Rötelstein*, Westweg branches to the right and starts to zigzag up the hill to *Beim Rötelsteinfelsen*. Fork to the right, and after passing a big tree that has been cut for passage continue to the right on a skinny little trail that skirts the edge of the hill. (This fork is easily missed!) ▶

After a tight bend the trail meets another track and briefly continues to the left, then branches to the right onto another small path that leads up to *Forsthütte*. Join the forest road to the left to *Dängeligeistweg* and take the small path to the left, down the hill. At turn right, past a lookout and down the hill to *Grenzach/Bettinger Straße*.

Turn right and at the next corner follow Erlenweg to Talstraße. Turn right and at the following corner left again on Auweg. At the end of Auweg take the steps down to Im Proli and turn right through the suburban fringe of Grenzach. After passing an orchard head back into the

This lovely narrow trail runs right along the stream and can be dangerous after heavy rains.

This path is quite jungly and may be difficult or dangerous in wet conditions.

Follow Swiss trail markings from Hornfelsen to the station

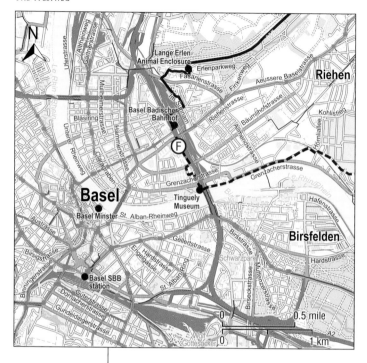

forest, and by *Schützenhaus* follow a small path up the hill towards Hornfelsen.

At *Am Hornfelsen* take a sharp right, quite steeply up to **Hornfelsen** (375m), where a picnic hut overlooks the Rhine, right on the Swiss border. Here the yellow Swiss trail markers take over.

Take the steep, small path down the hill to reach a paved lane on the edge of **Grenzach**. Bear right towards the benches and then turn left (Hirtenweg) to a T-junction. Turn left (Hörnliallee), cross the street and after passing under the bridge follow Bettingerweg along the tracks and around to the left, past a football field. Turn right on Grenzacherstraße, along the Rhine.

Where Grenzacherstraße bends to the right, Westweg continues straight on, through a small park to a subway that leads to the **Tinguely museum**. Turn right, cross Grenzacherstraße, bear left and take the first street to the right to follow Schwarzwaldallee to the **station** (Badischer Bahnhof), where Westweg ends.

BASEL

Basel is an intriguing city – beautiful, old, bustling and hip – and to really appreciate it you need to head for the old town, which lies on the other side of the Rhine. The area around Badische Bahnhof is not exactly charming, but if you keep walking straight, along the river past the Tinguely museum, you will soon come to another bridge, which leads right into the heart of the old town. Many of the historic sites, great art galleries and museums can easily be explored on foot; the tourist information office has a brochure available in English that outlines several walking routes, which are also waymarked for easy navigation through town.

Tourist Information Basel: at the Stadtcasino, at Barfüsserplatz or at the SBB train station, tel +41 (0)61 2686868, info@basel.com, **www.basel.com/en/tourist-information**

APPENDIX A

Route summary table

Stage	Start/Finish	Distance (km)	Ascent/ Descent (m)	Time	Page
1	Pforzheim (Kupferhammer)/Dobel	24.6	705/265	7–8hr	44
2	Dobel/Forbach	25.6	590/960	7hr	59
3	Forbach/Unterstmatt	19.6	1020/380	6hr	68
4	Unterstmatt/ Alexanderschanze	27.8	700/650	8hr	77
5	Alexanderschanze/Hark	17.1	290/550	5hr	87
6	Hark/Hausach	16	320/780	5hr	92
7	Hausach/Wilhelmshöhe	20.2	1135/400	6hr 30min	102
8	Wilhelmshöhe/Kalte Herberge	22.7	450/405	6hr	112
9	Kalte Herberge/Titisee	20.3	330/500	5hr 30min	121
Western route					
10A	Titisee/Notschrei	25.6	850/580	7hr 30min	130
11A	Notschrei/Haldenhof	18.9	605/790	5hr 30min	141
12A	Haldenhof/Kandern	19.8	470/1050	5hr	147
13A	Kandern/Basel	26.4	480/565	6hr 30min	156
Eastern route					
10B	Titisee/Feldbergpass	14.4	541/164	4hr 30min	168
11B	Feldbergpass/ Weißenbachsattel	18.5	720/875	5hr	175
12B	Weißenbachsattel/Hasel	22	345/980	5hr 30min	181
13B	Hasel/Degerfelden	24.4	410/545	6hr	189
14B	Degerfelden/Basel	17.3	390/425	5hr	199

APPENDIX B
Accommodation

Stage 1: Pforzheim to Dobel

Pforzheim

Parkhotel Pforzheim
Deimlingstraße 32–36
75175 Pforzheim
tel +49 (0)7231 1610
info@parkhotel-pforzheim.de
www.parkhotel-pforzheim.de/en/home

Hotel Gute Hoffnung
Dillsteiner Straße 9–11
75173 Pforzheim
tel +49 (0)7231 92290
info@hotel-gutehoffnung.com
www.hotel-gutehoffnung.com

Neuenbürg an der Enz

Wanderheim am Schlossberg
Hintere Schlosssteige 34
75305 Neuenbürg
tel +49 (0)7082 9444680
info@wanderheimamschlossberg.de
www.wanderheimamschlossberg.de

Straubenhardt

Silence Hotel Adlerhof
Mönchstraße. 14
75334 Straubenhardt
tel +49 (0)7082 92340
info@adlerhof.de
www.adlerhof.de

Dobel

Hotel Pension Heidi
Neuenbürgerstraße. 27
75335 Dobel
tel +49 (0)7083 2925

hotel-heidi@grambart.de
www.hotel-heidi.de

Gasthof zur Linde
Hauptstraße 19
75335 Dobel
tel +49 (0)7083 8873
info@linde-dobel.de
www.linde-dobel.de

Hotel-Restaurant Talblick
Wildbader Straße 63
75335 Dobel
tel +49 (0)7083 8806
info@talblick-dobel.de
www.talblick-dobel.de

Hotel-Restaurant Wagnerstüble
Wildbader Straße 45/1
75335 Dobel
tel +49 (0)7083 8758
info@roykieferle.de
www.roykieferle.de

Pension Beck
Wildbader Straße 30
75335 Dobel
tel +49 (0)7083 8828
kontakt@pension-beck.com
www.pension-beck.com

Stage 2: Dobel to Forbach

Kaltenbronn

Hotel Sarbacher
Kaltenbronner Straße 598
76593 Gernsbach-Kaltenbronn
tel +49 (0)7224 93390
info@hotel-sarbacher.de
www.hotel-sarbacher.de

Gausbach
Landgasthof Waldhorn
Murgtalstraße 67
76596 Forbach-Gausbach
tel +49 (0)7228 91870
info@landgasthof-waldhorn.de
www.landgasthof-waldhorn.de

Forbach
Hotel-Pension am Mühlbach
Mühlbachweg 4
76596 Forbach
tel +49 (0)7228 96970
info@hotel-am-muehlbach.com
www.hotel-am-muehlbach.com

Stage 3: Forbach to Unterstmatt

Badener Höhe
Naturfreundehaus Badener Höhe
Schwarzwaldhochstraße
77815 Bühl/Baden
tel +49 (0)7226 238
www.naturfreunde-karlsruhe.de/
haeuser/badener-hoehe
(closed during the winter season)

Bergwaldhütte Sand
Stadtwald 2a Schwarzwaldhochstraße
77815 Bühl-Sand
tel +49 (0)7226 237
bergwaldhuette@t-online.de
www.bergwaldhuettesand.de

Unterstmatt
Berggasthof Hochkopf-Stub
Raue Halde 6
77815 Bühl-Unterstmatt
tel +49 (0)7226 289
hochkopf-stub@t-online.de
www.hochkopf.de

Zur Großen Tanne
Unterstmatt 1
77815 Bühl-Unterstmatt
tel +49 (0)7226 254
zurgrossentanne@web.de
www.zurgrossentanne.de

Along the way, described in next stage
Ski-und Wanderheim Ochsenstall
Hundsrücken 1
77815 Bühl/Schwarzwaldhochstraße
tel +49 (0)7226 920911
info@wanderheim-ochsenstall.de
www.wanderheim-ochsenstall.de

Berghotel Mummelsee
Schwarzwaldhochstraße 11
77889 Seebach/Mummelsee
tel +49 (0)7842 99286
info@mummelsee.de
www.mummelsee.de

Stage 4: Unterstmatt to Alexanderschanze

Along the way
Darmstädter Hütte
Schwarzwaldhochstraße 5
77889 Seebach
tel +49 (0)7842 2247
info@darmstaedter-huette.de
www.darmstaedter-huette.de

Schliffkopf Wellness Hotel
Schwarzwaldhochstraße 1
72270 Baiersbronn-Schliffkopf
info@schliffkopf.de
www.schliffkopf.de

Natur und Sport Hotel Zuflucht
Zuflucht 1
72250 Freudenstadt
tel +49 (0)7804 912560
info@hotel-zuflucht.de
www.hotel-zuflucht.de

Kniebis
Hotel Schwarzwald Kniebis
Rippoldsauer Straße 53
72250 Freudenstadt
tel +49 (0)7442 180090
mail@schwarzwald-kniebis.de
www.hotel-schwarzwald-kniebis.de

Hotel Waldblick Kniebis
Eichelbachstraße 47
72250 Freudenstadt-Kniebis
tel +49 (0)7442 8340
info@waldblick-kniebis.de
www.waldblick-kniebis.de

Hotel Café Günter
Baiersbronner Sträßle 26
72250 Freudenstadt-Kniebis
tel +49 (0)7442 84130
cafe-guenter@t-online.de
www.cafe-guenter.de

Schwyzer-Stübli
Baiersbronner Straße 65
72250 Freudenstadt-Kniebis
tel +49 (0)7442 3683
schwyzer-stuebli@web.de
www.schwyzer-stuebli.de

Bad Peterstal-Griesbach
Höhengasthaus Herbstwasen
Wilde Rench 48
77740 Bad Peterstal-Griesbach
tel +49 (0)7806 627
gasthausherbstwasen@t-online.de
www.herbstwasen.de

Stage 5: Alexanderschanze to Hark

Hark
Harkhof
Hark 1
77784 Oberhamersbach
tel +49 (0)7837 835
vesperstube.hark@web.de
www.harkhof.de

Route described in next stage:
Wanderheim Brandenkopf
Brandenkopf 1
77784 Oberhamersbach
tel +49 (0)7831 6149
info@brandenkopf.net
www.brandenkopf.net

Stage 6: Hark to Hausach
Gasthaus Blume
Eisenbahnstraße 26
77756 Hausach
tel +49 (0)7831 286
pastor@hotelblume.de
www.hotelblume.de

Hotel Gasthaus zur Eiche
Gustav-Rivinius-Platz 1
77756 Hausach
tel +49 (0)7831 229
info@eiche-hausach.de
www.eiche-hausach.de

Gasthaus Zum Hirsch
Einbacher Straße 65
77756 Hausach
tel +49 (0)7831 7190 or 1401
info@gasthaus-hirsch-einbach.de
www.gasthaus-hirsch-einbach.de

Stage 7: Hausach to Wilhelmshöhe
Schöne Aussicht
Schöne Aussicht 1
78132 Hornberg
tel +49 (0)7833 93690
info@schoeneaussicht.com
www.schoeneaussicht.com

Vesperstube Silberberg
78136 Schonach
Fam. Fischer
tel +49 (0)7722 6564
urban.fischer@t-online.de
www.fischer-silberberg.de

Gasthaus Pension Wilhelmshöhe
Lukas-Kuner-Weg 1
78136 Schonach
tel +49 (0)7722 3293
info@gasthaus-wilhelmshoehe.de
www.gasthaus-wilhelmshoehe.de

Stage 8: Wilhelmshöhe to Kalte Herberge

Along the way

Kolmenhof an der Donauquelle
Neuweg 11
78120 Furtwangen
tel +49 (0)7723 93100
info@kolmenhof.de
www.kolmenhof.de

Naturfreundehaus Brend
Auf dem Brend 7
78120 Furtwangen
tel +49 (0)7723 803
nfh.brend@t-online.de
www.naturfreundehaus-brend.de

Hotel Goldener Rabe
Raben 7
78120 Furtwangen
tel +49 (0)7723 7397
www.goldener-rabe.de

Landgasthof zum Hirschen
Oberbregenbach 1
78120 Furtwangen/Neukirch
tel +49 (0)7723 7412
info@gasthaus-hirschen.de
www.gasthaus-hirschen.de

Höhengasthaus Kalte Herberge
Urachtalstraße 50
78147 Vöhrenbach
tel +49 (0)7723 7389
kalte.herberge@t-online.de
www.kalte-herberge.de

Stage 9: Kalte Herberge to Titisee

Titisee

Gasthaus Rehwinkel
Neustädterstraße 7
79822 Titisee-Neustadt
tel +49 (0)7651 8341
www.gasthaus-rehwinkel.de

Action Forest Active Hotel Garni
Neustädter Straße 41
79822 Titisee-Neustadt
tel +49 (0)7651 8256-0
hotel@action-forest.de
www.action-forest-hotel.de

Wald & See
Alte Poststraße 14
79822 Titisee-Neustadt
tel +49 (0)7651 8389
info@waldundsee.de
www.waldundsee.de/en/

A bit further along (route described in Stage 10A):

Hinterzarten

Hotel Imbery
Rathausstraße 14
79856 Hinterzarten
tel +49 (0)7652 91030

Gästehaus Schwarzwaldhüsle
Sickingerstraße 34
79856 Hinterzarten
tel +49 (0)7652 919677
info@gaestehaus-schwarzwaldhuesle.de
www.gaestehaus-schwarzwaldhuesle.de

Hotel am Bach
Windeckweg 9
79856 Hinterzarten
tel +49 (0)7652 286
info@hotel-am-bach.de

Bärental
Hotel Diana
Panoramaweg 11
79868 Feldberg-Bärental
tel +49 (0)7655 9396
hotel_diana@t-online.de
www.hotel-diana-feldberg.de

Hotel Tannhof
Im Dobel 1
79868 Feldberg-Bärental
tel +49 (0)7655 93320
info@tannhof-feldberg.de
www.tannhof-feldberg.de

Western route

Stage 10A: Titisee to Notschrei
Berggasthaus Stübenwasen
Stübenwasen 1
79674 Todtnau
tel +49 (0)7671 334
info@berggasthof-stuebenwasen.de
www.berggasthof-stuebenwasen.de

Waldhotel am Notschrei
Notschrei Passhöhe 2
79674 Todtnau
tel +49 (0)7602 9420
info@waldhotel-am-Notschrei.de
www.waldhotel-am-notschrei.de

Muggenbrunn
Vital Hotel Grüner Baum
Schauinslandstraße 3
79674 Todtnau-Muggenbrunn
tel +49 (0)7671 918440
info@gruener-baum-todtnau.de
schwarzwald-vitalhotel.de

Oberried
Hotel die Halde
Halde 2
79254 Oberried
tel +49 (0)7602 94470

Stage 11A: Notschrei to Haldenhof
Belchenhotel Jägerstüble (by the cable
car base station)
Obermulten 3
79677 Aitern-Multen
tel +49 (0)7673 888180
info@belchenhotel.de
www.belchenhotel.de

Berggasthof Haldenhof
Haldenhof 1
79692 Kleines Wiesental/Ortsteil
Neuenweg
tel +49 7673 284
haldenhof@aol.com
www.haldenhof-schwarzwald.de

Stage 12A: Haldenhof to Kandern
Historisches Gasthaus und Hotel 'Zur
Weserei'
Hauptstraße 81
79400 Kandern
tel +49 (0)7626 445
info@weserei.de
www.weserei.de

Gasthaus zur Schnecke
Ziegelstraße 8
79400 Kandern
tel +49 (0)7626 8303
hotel@zur-schnecke.de
www.zur-schnecke.de

Stage 13A: Kandern to Basel

Basel
Der Teufelhof
Leonhardsgraben 49
Basel 4051
Switzerland
tel +41 61 588 0169
info@teufelhof.com
www.teufelhof.com/en/hotel

Hotel Spalentor
Schönbeinstraße 1
Basel 4056
Switzerland
tel +41 61 588 0626
info@hotelspalentor.ch
www.hotelspalentor.ch/en

Gaia Hotel
Centralbahnstraße 13–15
Basel 4002
Switzerland
tel +41 61 225 1313
welcome@gaiahotel.ch
www.gaiahotel.ch/en/home

Apaliving Basel
J.J. Balmer Straße 1
Basel 4053
Switzerland
tel +41 61 333 0530
info@apaliving.ch
www.apaliving.ch/en/basel-hotel

IBIS Basel Bahnhof
Margarethenstraße 33–35
Basel 4053
Switzerland
tel +41 61 201 0707
h6510@accor.com
www.accorhotels.com

Lörrach

Stadthotel Lörrach
Weinbrennerstraße 2
79539 Lörrach
tel +49 (0)7621 40090
info@stadthotel-loerrach.de
www.stadthotel-loerrach.de

Eastern route

Stage 10B: Titisee to Feldberg

Berghotel Jägermatt
Am Seebuck 1
79868 Feldberg
tel +49 (0)7676 92620
berghotel-jaegermatt@t-online.de
www.berghotel-jaegermatt.de

Berggasthaus Emmendinger Hütte
Grafenmattweg 3
79868 Feldberg-Ort
tel +49 (0)7676 236
post@emmendinger-huette.de
www.emmendinger-huette.de

Stage 11B: Feldberg to Weißenbachsattel

Hotel Hochkopfhaus zum Auerhahn
Hochkopf 1
79674 Todtnau
tel +49 (0) 7674 437
waldrestaurant-auerhahn@t-online.de
www.hochkopfhaus-auerhahn.de

Romantisches Schwarzwaldhotel
Alte Dorfstraße 29
79682 Todtmoos-Weg
tel +49 (0) 7674 9053-0
info@romantisches-schwarzwaldhotel.de
www.romantisches-schwarzwaldhotel.de/

Stage 12B: Weißenbachsattel to Hasel

Schweigmatt
Berggasthaus Waldhaus
Schweigmatt 11
79650 Schopfheim
tel +49 (0)7622 683956
berggasthaus-waldhaus@t-online.de
www.berggasthof-waldhaus.de

Hasel
Landgasthof Erdmannshöhle
Hauptstraße 14
79686 Hasel
tel +49 (0)7762 5218-0
info@erdmannshoehle.de
www.erdmannshoehle.de

Stage 13B: Hasel to Degerfelden
Landgasthaus Hotel Maien
Maienplatz 2
79618 Rheinfelden Ober-Eichsel
tel +49 (0)7623 7215-0
info@gasthaus-maien.de
www.gasthaus-maien.de

(For Stage 14B see Stage 13A listings
in Basel)

APPENDIX C
Further information

There are practically no useful books about the Black Forest available in English. Lonely Planet publishes a guide to *Munich, Bavaria & the Black Forest* (4th edition, 2013) and Rough Guides has a kindle edition that focuses on the Black Forest (*Rough Guides Snapshot Germany: The Black Forest* (2015)). Locally widely available, *Black Forest: Markgräflerland, Kaiserstuhl and Freiburg* (Schoening Und Co, 2009), by Christopher Watson, offers brief background information but is not very useful as a guidebook.

If you do not speak any German it would certainly be a good idea to equip yourself with a phrasebook or dictionary. Lonely Planet publishes *Fast Talk German* (2nd edition, 2013), which is quite good – even though the local dialect doesn't resemble 'high German' much, people will be able to understand it.

Tourist information offices
Black Forest Tourist Board (Schwarzwald Tourismus GmbH)

Main office (Freiburg):
Heinrich-von-Stephan-Straße 8b
79100 Freiburg
tel +49 (0)761 896460
fax +49 (0)761 8964670
mail@schwarzwald-tourismus.info
www.schwarzwald-tourismus.info

Pforzheim branch:
Am Waisenhausplatz 26
75172 Pforzheim
tel +49 (0)7231 147380
fax +49 (0)7231 1473820
touristik@schwarzwald-tourismus.info

Stage 1

Pforzheim
Tourist Information Pforzheim
Schloßberg 15–17
75175 Pforzheim
tel +49 (0)7231 393700
tourist-info@ws-pforzheim.de

Dobel
Tourismusbüro Dobel
Neue Herrenalber Straße 11
75335 Dobel
tel +49 (0)7083 74513
kontakt@dobel.info
www.dobel.de/gaeste/
tourist-information

Stage 2

Forbach
Rathaus Forbach
Landstraße 27
76596 Forbach
tel +49 (0)7228 390
touristinfo@forbach.de
www.forbach.de

Stage 3

Bühl
Hauptstraße 47
77815 Bühl
tel +49 (0)7223 935332
tourist.info@buehl.de
www.buehl.de

Bühlertal
Hauptstraße 92
77830 Bühlertal
tel +49 (0)7223 99670
tourist.info@buehlertal.de
www.buehlertal.de

Stage 4

Kniebis
Besucherzentrum Schwarzwaldhochstraße Freudenstadt-Kniebis
Straßburger Straße 349
72250 Freudenstadt-Kniebis
tel +49 (0)7442 7570
info@kniebis.de
www.kniebis.de

Stage 6

Oberharmersbach
Dorf 60
77784 Oberharmersbach
tel +49 (0)7837 277
tourist-info@oberharmersbach.net
www.oberharmersbach.de

Hausach
Hauptstraße 40
77756 Hausach
tel +49 (0)7831 7975
tourist-info@hausach.de
www.hausach.de

Stage 7

Schonach
Haus des Gastes
Hauptstraße 6
78136 Schonach im Schwarzwald
tel +49 (0)7722 964810
info@schonach.de
www.schonach.de

Stage 8

Vöhrenbach
78147 Vöhrenbach
tel +49 (0)7727 501115
info@voehrenbach.de
www.voehrenbach.de

Stage 9

Titisee
Strandbadstraße 4
79822 Titisee-Neustadt
tel +49 (0)7652 12068100
titisee@hochschwarzwald.de
www.titisee-neustadt.de

Stage 10A

Hinterzarten
Freiburger Straße 1
79856 Hinterzarten
tel +49 (0)7652 12068200
hinterzarten@hochschwarzwald.de
www.hochschwarzwald.de

Stage 11A

Badenweiler
Schlossplatz 2
79410 Badenweiler
tel +49 7632 799300
touristik@badenweiler.de
www.badenweiler.de

Stage 12A

Kandern
79400 Kandern
tel +49 (0)7626 972356
verkehrsamt@kandern.de
www.kandern.de

Stage 13A

Basel
At the Stadtcasino, at Barfüsserplatz or
at the SBB train station
tel +41 (0)61 2686868
info@basel.com
www.basel.com/en/tourist-information

Stage 10B

Feldberg
Dr.-Pilet-Spur 4
79868 Feldberg (Schwarzwald
tel +49 (0)7652 1206-0
feldberg@hochschwarzwald.de
www.hochschwarzwald.de/Feldberg

Stage 11B

Todtmoos
Wehratalstraße 19
79682 Todtmoos
tel +49 (0) 7674 9060-0
info@todtmoos.net
www.todtmoos.de

Stage 12B

Schopfheim
Hauptstraße 23
79650 Schopfheim
tel +49 (0)7622 396145
tourismus@schopfheim.de
www.schopfheim.de

Stage 13B

Rheinfelden (Germany)
Karl-Fürstenberg-Straße 17
79618 Rheinfelden (Baden)
tel +49 (0)7623 9668720
info@tourismus-rheinfelden.de
www.rheinfelden.de/en/Tourism

Rheinfelden (Switzerland)
Stadtbüro
Marktgasse 16
4310 Rheinfelden
tel +41 (0) 61 8355200
tourismus@rheinfelden.ch
www.tourismus-rheinfelden.ch

Transport

Air
Basel airport
www.euroairport.com

Stuttgart airport
www.stuttgart-airport.com

Frankfurt airport
www.frankfurt-airport.com

Train and bus
The best journey planners for
smartphones, available from the Google
Play shop, are Öffi and EVA_BW.

Deutsche Bahn
www.bahn.de

NVBW (local transport journey planner)
www.efa-bw.de

Weather
Wetter.info or wetter.com are the best
weather sites (although they often differ
in their prognosis). Wetter.info publishes
a useful app, as well as a rain radar app.

Emergency numbers
Police/Emergency 110
Fire brigade/ambulance 112
Poison helpline 0761 192 40

APPENDIX D
German–English glossary

Local and topographical features

German	English
Gemeinde	Community
Haltestelle	Bus or train stop
Hbf	Main train station (abbreviation of Hauptbahnhof)
ZOB	Central bus station (Zentraler Omnibus Bahnhof)
Kirche	Church
Kapelle	Chapel
Friedhof	Cemetery
Rathaus	Town hall
Brücke	Bridge
Bach/Bächle	Stream
Fluss	River
Matten	Pasture
Mühle	Mill
Buck	Hillock
Bannwald	Forest reserve (in Baden-Württemberg)
Alm	Mountain farmstead
Steg	Footbridge
Steig	Small ascending trail
Weg	Way, trail
Wanderweg	Hiking trail
Wanderparkplatz	Car park with access to trails
Hock	Village fete

Eating out

German	English
Almgasthof/Almgaststätte	Mountain restaurant/café
Besenwirtschaft/Straußi	Farmhouse restaurant (open seasonally)
Vesper	Colloquial term meaning 'snack'
Vesperstube	Snack bar
Vesperkarte	Snack menu

Unusual items you might find on the menu

Brägele	Fried potatoes
Gschwelldi	Boiled potatoes (with skin)
Bibbeleskäs	Smooth cottage cheese (like fromage blanc)
Kartoffelsalat	Potato salad
Wurstsalad	Meat salad (sausage)
Spätzle	Local pasta speciality, usually topped with cheese
Knöpfle	Similar to Spätzle, but pasta is 'button-shaped'
Schupfnudeln	Similar to gnocchi
Zwiebelkuchen or Zwiebelwaie	Onion pie, a seasonal dish usually served in the autumn with 'Neuer Süßer', a sweet and fizzy, slightly fermented grape juice
Schäufele	Pork shoulder
Flammkuchen	Alsatian pizza with an extremely thin and crisp crust, spread with crème fraîche and toppings such as spinach and salmon, leeks and bacon bits or tomatoes and feta cheese – there are many permutations on the theme.
Schwarzwälder Schinken	Cured, smoked ham (regional speciality)
Bärlauch	Wild garlic. Many restaurants offer Bärlauch dishes as a seasonal speciality in spring.
Viertele	A quarter litre of wine
Schwarzwälderkirschtorte	Black Forest Gateau. This rich creamy chocolate-cherry gateau has gained worldwide fame. It really did originate in the Black Forest and most cafés serve wonderful home-made versions. Careful though – it often comes in monstrously sized slices and heavily laced with Kirsch brandy.
Brennerei	Distillery

NOTES

LISTING OF CICERONE GUIDES

Scrambles in the Lake District
– South
Short Walks in Lakeland
Book 1: South Lakeland
Short Walks in Lakeland
Book 2: North Lakeland
Short Walks in Lakeland
Book 3: West Lakeland
The Cumbria Coastal Way
The Cumbria Way
Tour of the Lake District

DERBYSHIRE, PEAK DISTRICT AND MIDLANDS

High Peak Walks
Scrambles in the Dark Peak
Walking in Derbyshire
White Peak Walks:
The Northern Dales
White Peak Walks:
The Southern Dales

SOUTHERN ENGLAND

The Cotswold Way
The Cotswold Way Map Booklet
The Great Stones Way
The Kennet and Avon Canal
The Lea Valley Walk
The North Downs Way
The Peddars Way and Norfolk
Coast Path
The Ridgeway Map Booklet
The Ridgeway National Trail
The South Downs Way
The South West Coast Path
The Thames Path
The Thames Path Map Booklet
The Two Moors Way
Walking in Cornwall
Walking in Essex
Walking in Kent
Walking in Norfolk
Walking in Sussex
Walking in the Chilterns
Walking in the Cotswolds
Walking in the Isles of Scilly
Walking in the New Forest
Walking in the North
Wessex Downs
Walking in the Thames Valley
Walking on Dartmoor
Walking on Guernsey
Walking on Jersey
Walking on the Isle of Wight
Walking the Jurassic Coast
Walks in the South Downs
National Park

WALES AND WELSH BORDERS

Glyndwr's Way

Great Mountain Days in
Snowdonia
Hillwalking in Shropshire
Hillwalking in Wales – Vol 1
Hillwalking in Wales – Vol 2
Mountain Walking in Snowdonia
Offa's Dyke Path
Offa's Dyke Path Map Booklet
Pembrokeshire Coast Path
Map Booklet
Ridges of Snowdonia
Scrambles in Snowdonia
The Ascent of Snowdon
The Ceredigion and Snowdonia
Coast Paths
The Pembrokeshire Coast Path
The Severn Way
The Wales Coast Path
The Wye Valley Walk
Walking in Carmarthenshire
Walking in Pembrokeshire
Walking in the Forest of Dean
Walking in the South
Wales Valleys
Walking in the Wye Valley
Walking on the Brecon Beacons
Walking on the Gower
Welsh Winter Climbs

INTERNATIONAL CHALLENGES, COLLECTIONS AND ACTIVITIES

Canyoning in the Alps
The Via Francigena
Canterbury to Rome – Part 1
The Via Francigena
Canterbury to Rome – Part 2

EUROPEAN CYCLING

Cycle Touring in France
Cycle Touring in Spain
Cycle Touring in Switzerland
Cycling in the French Alps
Cycling the Canal du Midi
Cycling the River Loire
The Danube Cycleway Volume 1
The Danube Cycleway Volume 2
The Grand Traverse of the
Massif Central
The Moselle Cycle Route
The Rhine Cycle Route
The River Rhone Cycle Route
The Way of St James
Cyclist Guide

PYRENEES AND FRANCE/SPAIN CROSS BORDER ROUTES

100 Hut Walks in the Alps
Across the Eastern Alps: E5
Alpine Ski Mountaineering Vol 1
– Western Alps

Alpine Ski Mountaineering Vol 2
– Central and Eastern Alps
Chamonix to Zermatt
The Tour of the Bernina
Tour of Mont Blanc
Tour of Monte Rosa
Tour of the Matterhorn
Trail Running – Chamonix and
the Mont Blanc region
Trekking in the Alps
Trekking in the Silvretta and
Rätikon Alps
Trekking Munich to Venice
Walking in the Alps

PYRENEES AND FRANCE/SPAIN CROSS BORDER ROUTES

The GR10 Trail
The GR11 Trail – La Senda
The Mountains of Andorra
The Pyrenean Haute Route
The Pyrenees
The Way of St James – France
The Way of St James – Spain
Walks and Climbs in the Pyrenees

AUSTRIA

The Adlerweg
Trekking in Austria's Hohe Tauern
Trekking in the Stubai Alps
Trekking in the Zillertal Alps
Walking in Austria

BELGIUM AND LUXEMBOURG

Walking in the Ardennes

EASTERN EUROPE

The High Tatras
The Mountains of Romania
Walking in Bulgaria's
National Parks
Walking in Hungary

FRANCE

Chamonix Mountain Adventures
Ecrins National Park
Mont Blanc Walks
Mountain Adventures in
the Maurienne
The Cathar Way
The GR20 Corsica
The GR5 Trail
The Robert Louis Stevenson Trail
Tour of the Oisans: The GR54
Tour of the Queyras
Tour of the Vanoise
Vanoise Ski Touring
Via Ferratas of the French Alps
Walking in Corsica
Walking in Provence – East

For full information on all our guides, books and eBooks, visit our website:
www.cicerone.co.uk

Walking – Trekking – Mountaineering – Climbing – Cycling

Over 40 years, Cicerone have built up an outstanding collection of over 300 guides, inspiring all sorts of amazing adventures.

Every guide comes from extensive exploration and research by our expert authors, all with a passion for their subjects. They are frequently praised, endorsed and used by clubs, instructors and outdoor organisations.

All our titles can now be bought as **e-books**, **ePubs** and **Kindle** files and we also have an online magazine – **Cicerone Extra** – with features to help cyclists, climbers, walkers and trekkers choose their next adventure, at home or abroad.

Our website shows any **new information** we've had in since a book was published. Please do let us know if you find anything has changed, so that we can publish the latest details. On our **website** you'll also find great ideas and lots of detailed information about what's inside every guide and you can buy **individual routes** from many of them online.

It's easy to keep in touch with what's going on at Cicerone by getting our monthly **free e-newsletter**, which is full of offers, competitions, up-to-date information and topical articles. You can subscribe on our home page and also follow us on **Facebook** and **Twitter** or dip into our **blog**.

Cicerone – the very best guides for exploring the world.

CICERONE

2 Police Square Milnthorpe Cumbria LA7 7PY
Tel: 015395 62069 info@cicerone.co.uk
www.cicerone.co.uk and **www.cicerone-extra.com**